What Leaders Are Saying

"This book can help you unload any extra baggage that is weighing you down. The message is right on time!"

> Pastor Billy Joe Daugherty,
> Victory Christian Center, Tulsa

"This is not just a book every person should read; it is a book we should all have on hand to give away to those we love who are dealing with bitterness and unforgiveness."

> from the foreword by Jimmy Evans,
> president and founder, Marriage Today

"Duane Vander Klok is practical, powerful and persuasive. You will not only love this book; you will change with it. It brings an insightful truth that will set you free!"

> Casey Treat, senior pastor,
> Christian Faith Center, Seattle

"Anyone whose heart cries out, *God, help me! I'm so tired of being paralyzed by the bad memories of my past!* needs to read this life-changing and freedom-imparting book. As I read it, I was gripped by the vast number of people who can't effectively live today because they are still clinging to the memories of yesterday. How tragic, for there is so much life to be lived right now! Do you want to leave your past behind once and for all so you can fully live for today as you pursue God's good plan for your future? If so, I recommend that you read this book immediately!"

> Rick Renner, president, Rick Renner Ministries;
> president, Good News Association of Pastors and
> Churches; pastor, Moscow Good News Church

"Excess baggage only makes the load heavier. We could not agree more with Pastor Duane and have seen firsthand that his wisdom and insight can help those who read this to move forward and grow to a higher level in God. This book reminds us of a saying we have had in our ministry for years: 'When driving down the road of life, rip off the rearview mirror!' You can't go forward looking back, and the 'junk in your trunk' can only impede your progress going forward."

Harry and Cheryl Salem, founders,
Salem Family Ministries

"You and I have a decision to make—whether to stay in the suffocating wilderness of bitterness or to get better. Pastor Vander Klok lays out a blueprint for overcoming a stronghold that keeps leaders from leading and, more importantly, keeps people from an intimate relationship with God. What a vision—to utilize God's amazing grace to find the ultimate treasure and live a life of genuine forgiveness."

William V. Crouch, president,
Van Crouch Communications

"A must-read for everyone. All of us have been hurt and all of us know we are supposed to forgive, but how do we forgive? We can't take one step forward today or tomorrow until we let go of yesterday. Pastor Duane Vander Klok shows us *how* to forgive so we can get our lives unstuck and fulfill the destiny God has for us. His kind, sympathetic and humorous presentation is riveting. You won't be able to put this book down!"

Robert Morris, senior pastor,
Gateway Church, Southlake, Texas

GET THE

JUNK
OUT OF YOUR
TRUNK

Let Go of the Past
to Live Your Best Life

λ

DUANE VANDER KLOK

Chosen
Grand Rapids, Michigan

Published by Chosen Books
a division of Baker Publishing Group
P.O. Box 6287, Grand Rapids, MI 49516-6287

Printed in the United States of America

Library of Congress Cataloging-in-Publication Data
Vander Klok, Duane, 1953–
    Get the junk out of your trunk : let go of the past to live your best life /
Duane Vander Klok.
        p.   cm.
    ISBN 0-8007-9399-4 (pbk.)
    1. Christian life. 2. Peace of mind—Religious aspects—Christianity. I. Title.
BV4501.3.V36 2005
248.4—dc22   2005009920

I dedicate this book to my wife,
Jeanie,
with whom I am living an
adventurous life of faith
and forgiveness

Contents

Acknowledgments

I am grateful to John Nardini for having the vision to see this teaching on forgiveness in book form, for initiating the necessary contacts to make it happen and for encouraging me in the process.

My thanks also to Trish Konieczny for her countless hours of meticulous labor over the manuscript and revisions.

Without John it wouldn't have happened. Without Trish it couldn't have happened.

I also appreciate:

Jane Campbell, Editorial Director of Chosen Books, for her invaluable guidance and enthusiasm;

Paulette Albrecht for her fast and accurate transcription services; and

Deb Aylworth and Jodi de Melo-Hanson, my assistants, for looking after the daily details.

Foreword

After 25 years of ministry, I have come to the conclusion that the primary issue that damages people's lives and keeps them from personal, emotional and relational fulfillment is bitterness. It is a universal issue that all of us must deal with in order to be free from the past and to be able to move forward in life.

Duane Vander Klok has been my friend for many years. Without a doubt he is the person to write this book about ridding yourself of toxic emotions and keeping your heart free from bitterness and unforgiveness. In many hours of real-life conversations with Duane—sometimes involving very difficult issues and "painful people"—I have never heard him utter a bitter word. Instead, he is a man full of grace who has learned the lesson well that he teaches in this powerful book.

As a gifted pastor and communicator, Duane Vander Klok has written a primer on a critical subject. This is not just a book every person should read; it is a book we should all have on hand to give away to those we love who are dealing with bitterness and unforgiveness.

Jimmy Evans
President and founder, Marriage Today

1

The High Price
of Living Low

Denise had a kind and decent husband who loved her. Her children loved her, too, and they had a fine home. God had a great life planned for her. Yet she was filing for divorce and walking away. . . .

Eric was drinking too much, and he knew it. He could see its effects on his wife, his job and his spiritual life. His kids were afraid of him. *I'm nothing like my dad, though!* Eric consoled himself. *The old man was the worst, most abusive drunkard. . . .*

Bill watched as evidence in the murder case pointed increasingly to his father's business associate. Finally it was conclusive: That vile person had actually hired someone to murder his father. Bill was livid when inadmissible evidence kept the hired man from being tried and punished, so he vowed that justice would be done. *Vengeance,* Bill thought, *is mine.* . . .

Different people, different circumstances, but they and countless others have paid the same high price—the high price of living low. They chose something that cost some their marriages, some their kids, some their jobs, their possessions, their peace of mind . . . even their lives. This low level of life is not worth the high price that it costs.

Just as a trunk full of junk will weigh you down, likewise, if you choose to keep junk in your heart it will take you down. It will cause you to live below your potential, deprive you of peace, steal your joy, keep you hopeless and ruin your relationships. It will keep you from your hopes and dreams as your energy is constantly drained trying to handle life with a trunk full of junk.

The trunk I am talking about was never meant to carry "junk." It is the place the Bible calls your heart. You can fill it with treasures—a God-given dream, a wonderful memory, the joy of a special relationship—things that fill you with deep satisfaction and thankfulness.

But you can also place trash there—junk that you are unwilling or have felt unable to deal with. If you have taken offense and hung on to it, you have put it in your trunk. If you are holding tightly to your hurts, they are taking up room in your trunk. If the pain in your past won't let go, it is along for the ride in your trunk. Living with junk in your trunk steals your peace, weighs you down and will eventually poison other areas of your life.

Anyone can accumulate a trunk full of junk. Jesus told us, "It is impossible that no offenses should come, but woe to him through whom they do come!" (Luke 17:1). In other words, we should not think it strange as we go through life that people mistreat us or criticize us or lie about us or abuse us or do any number of other things they should not do. Everyone experiences numerous opportunities to get offended—guaranteed. Stuff happens, and if we are not careful we are jamming our trunks full of every offense and hurt that comes our way.

Often, the people closest to us can become the source of our greatest hurts, which presents us with the easiest offenses to pick up. They have the most effect on us because we are the most open and vulnerable to them. If a person I don't know makes some very critical comments about my sermon, I can take the words, weigh their content, apply what is needed, throw out the rest and go on. *But*, if my wife were to say, "That was one terrible job of preaching you did today. . . . You looked bad, too. . . ." Now, *that* would knock me right off my feet. I would walk away with thoughts of disappointment, failure, rejection and hurt—a perfect setup to take offense and load up my own heart with bitter thoughts like: *She doesn't appreciate me. . . . She can't be pleased. . . . She always picks on me. . . . She's not so perfect either, in fact I remember how she failed. . . . And what a bad job she does . . . and . . .* It is amazing how one bit of "heart pollution" (or maybe better put, "hurt pollution") leads to another until our trunks become filled with it and our closest relationships are ruined. But we must and *can* forgive offenses even from those closest to us.

Offenses are like hazardous materials. My wife (being from the farm and having experience with cows) describes offenses as being "plopped on"—something we all would get cleaned off *immediately*. Yet, instead of putting offenses away from us, as we would a poop-filled diaper, we accept them—scooping them up, stuffing them into our pockets

15

and walking away with them. Then we blame others that our lives stink.

Maybe we stuff pride or self-deception into our trunks, or maybe we pack some mental torment or memories of a painful past. Whatever the offense, if we refuse to release it through an act of forgiveness, it will travel through life with us. Our hearts become polluted and we experience the toxic effects of bitterness: loss of peace and focus, loss of health, loss of our most important relationships. Unforgiveness and bitterness are hazardous and heavy burdens that we were not meant to carry through life. No wonder that under their oppressive weight we are destined to live a low life instead of the much better life God intended for us!

Jesus Traveled Light

What we choose to carry in our trunks can determine whether we take hold of that best life God has planned for us or struggle with the best always just out of reach. Jesus showed us how to avoid paying the high price of living low. He did not stuff junk in His trunk, even junk provided by those closest to Him. He did not pick up offenses or let them enter His heart. Throughout Jesus' ministry, Judas was at His side as one of the twelve closest to Him. When Judas betrayed Jesus with a kiss, Jesus simply called him "Friend" and forgave him! Even at the crucifixion Jesus forgave His offenders, and He prayed, "Father, forgive them, for they do not know what they do" (Luke 23:34). Jesus forgave everyone of everything—immediately.

When you can do the same, you are beginning to grow spiritually. Then when offenses come, they just roll off you like water off a duck's back. What happens when you pour water on a duck? You cannot get the duck wet! Pour a hundred gallons of water on a duck and he will stay dry. Those feathers keep the water flowing right off him. That should happen with offenses in our lives. They should roll right off us.

First Corinthians 13:5 says that love does not take into account a wrong that has been done to it, or in some translations, a wrong suffered. You can suffer a wrong and stuff it into your trunk. You can even try to convince other people to stuff it into their trunks, too, by telling them all about it: "He hurt me. And do you know what else he did?" Or you can walk in love. No matter what someone does, you let it roll off and you keep going. You put one foot down . . . someone treats you poorly . . . then by the time you put the next foot down you are saying, "Bless him, Lord." You have already forgiven the person and kept right on living your best life without allowing offense to slow you down.

No Junk, Know Peace

It is possible to get to a place where nothing offends you. You decide beforehand, as Jesus did, that you are *not* going to receive any offense, and then you keep yourself full of the Word of God. The psalmist wrote, "Great peace have they which love thy law: and nothing shall offend them" (Psalm 119:165, KJV). When the Bible says *nothing* it means *nothing*! If nothing offends you, you have great peace. Or to look at that another way, if offense enters your life, your peace is the first thing to go. You cannot have it both ways—you cannot be offended and have peace. You can carry offenses and have no peace, or you can let nothing offend you and have great peace. That is the place we all need to get to, where we don't take up offenses and nothing takes away our peace.

Peace is too important to live without, so important that when Jesus sent out His disciples He told them, "When you go into a household, greet it. If the household is worthy, let your peace come upon it. But if it is not worthy, let your peace return to you" (Matthew 10:12–13). Peace is a positive spiritual force, just as fear is a negative spiritual force. Most people never say, "Peace to this house," when they enter one, but Jesus said that peace will come on the place if we do. Why was this an important practice for the disciples when they went out to preach the Gospel? Because they needed a place to minister from—not just any place, but a place of peace.

As believers we are all ministers, so we all need a place of peace. In fact, not having a peaceful place to minister from cripples our ministry. If we do not have peace in our homes, we will be crippled in our ability to minister inside our homes and outside them, too.

Jesus wants us to have peace; without it, we stumble spiritually. The NKJV translates Psalm 119:165 this way: "Great peace have those who love Your law, and nothing causes them to stumble." Hebrews 12 compares the spiritual life to running a race. It is hard to run well when we are stumbling. When we let offense into our lives we are, in effect, tying our shoestrings together spiritually and trying to run. Letting resentment, unforgiveness and hatred into our lives will trip us up spiritually no matter how hard we try to go on!

If something keeps tripping you up or weighing you down in your spiritual race, it would be wise to check the contents of your trunk. Your heart might be too heavy because it is full of junk. You do not have to keep struggling, or even worse, drop out of the race altogether. You can experience release and enjoy freedom!

In the following chapters, I invite you to let the Word of God reveal the contents of your heart. If any junk does not belong there, we will learn how to take it out and leave it behind. The "Unloading Your Trunk" questions at the end of each chapter will help guide you through the process.

I invite you to take an honest look with me at any bitterness and its consequences that might occupy your trunk: junk stemming from painful memories and self-deception, unhealthy connections and unresolved anger, or poor spiritual and physical health. Let's talk about how bitter roots get started, how we can stop them before they cause trouble and what junk we end up carrying when we do not put a halt to them. Then we will expose junk habits such as complaining and spreading strife. We will face the poisonous thoughts of bitterness toward God. We will examine the importance of having a clear conscience and a junk-free trunk. And we will learn how we can genuinely forgive and possess the treasure of a heart full of peace—so we can live our best lives for God!

Some of the junk you discover in your trunk may seem difficult to face at first. It may seem like a permanent part of your being, but Jesus came to free you from the things that would destroy your life, your peace, your home and your future.

> He has sent Me to heal the brokenhearted, to proclaim liberty to the captives, and the opening of the prison to those who are bound; . . . to give them beauty for ashes, the oil of joy for mourning, the garment of praise for the spirit of heaviness.
>
> Isaiah 61:1, 3

God paid a great price to release you from the junk that would destroy you. He is all for you being junk free! If you want to know peace, minister effectively and run your spiritual race well, read on. Make certain that you are storing treasures in the trunk of your heart—and putting out the trash.

Unloading Your Trunk

1. Scripture talks often about the condition of our hearts. Proverbs 4:23 says: "Keep your heart with all diligence, for out of it spring the issues of life." Are you frustrated with some issues in your life—maybe they are "giving off a bad odor"? It is time to take out the trash!
2. Do you know someone who is full of enthusiasm and displays a zest for life? Can you think of someone else who is living low, barely able to make it through the day because life is such a heavy burden? Imagine placing the "trunks" of these people side by side and opening the lids. How do you think the contents would differ?
3. Do you feel like either of the people in question 2? Are you somewhere in between? Is your heart light or heavy, peaceful or troubled? Do you think that some of the contents there might be crowding out the peace and joy in your life? Let's start the process toward peace.

2

Letting Go of Yesterday

I watched the couple make their way down the aisle toward me after a church service and wondered if their approach might turn into a tug-of-war. His arm was stretched all the way out behind him, his hand gripping hers. Her arm was stretched all the way out in front of her, and she was leaning backward hard, resisting him, as he literally pulled her along. He kept a tight grip on her hand while they waited for me to talk with them.

I was standing in the front of the sanctuary and meeting people who came for prayer. When I worked my way over to this couple, I asked, "Can I help you?"

"Pastor, I need you to help my wife," the man said. "I need you to fix her!"

Fix her? I thought. "Tell me what's wrong," I said.

"She's divorcing me," he said in anguish.

"What did you do?"

"Pastor, I don't know that I've done *anything*."

I checked his story out with her. "Is it true you want a divorce?"

"Yes, it is," she said flatly.

"Why?"

"I hate him," she said, heatedly this time.

"What did he do?"

"He's a man," she said. "I hate men! I hate *all* men—I even hate you!"

She hates her husband, she hates men she has never even met, she hates me—a man must have done something to her, I thought. And it sure didn't take any special gift of discernment on my part to figure that out.

So I asked, "Did some man do something to hurt you, or did your husband hurt you?"

"No, no, *I just hate men!*" she spat.

Her anger was red-hot now, so I knew there was more to it. I continued to probe until it finally came out: When this woman, whom I will call "Denise," was a young girl, a family member had sexually abused her, and it went on for years.

She looked at me and said, "If I could, I would kill him."

I did not doubt her. Yet as I talked with the couple further, I saw that here was a woman in a situation many people long for: Her husband genuinely loved her, I learned, and her children loved her, too; it seemed evident that God had a great plan for her life. Yet every day she was turning her back on it all, ignoring the present to relive the agony, the reproach and the offense of what took place many years ago. And now she planned to walk away permanently. Denise could not grab hold of what God had for her today because her hands were too full of yesterday. She had packed her trunk full of painful memories and unforgiveness, and it was destroying the most valuable relationships in her life. She could not go on, but she could not see how to let go and forgive either.

If we could have the apostle Paul with us today and ask, "Paul, what do you consider to be the most important help for our spiritual lives?" I believe Paul would take us right to Philippians 3:13 and say, "This one thing I do, forgetting those things which are behind, and reaching forth unto those things which are before" (KJV).

Millions of people cannot live a great life today because they are still holding on to yesterday. In this passage Paul says to forget those things that are behind and reach ahead. If your trunk is full of painful memories and unforgiveness, your hands are full of yesterday. That makes it impossible to hold on to what God has for you today—and impossible to reach for what He has for you tomorrow.

I explained these things to Denise, then added, "Jesus said you need to forgive him."

"I just can't," she said.

"Jesus said you can," I insisted. I knew it seemed impossible to her, but I also knew that the unforgiveness in her trunk was seeping like poison into her system. My wife, Jeanie, always says at home that unforgiveness is like drinking poison and waiting for the other person to die.

Unforgiveness is poison, but it is poison in *your* system, not in the person's who wronged you. Half the time that person does not even know you are upset; he or she goes about his or her daily routine while you embrace all the pain. The poison of unforgiveness eats away at *your* life. It affects your today, and it will affect your tomorrows.

Who knew if Denise's abusive relative even gave her—or what he had done to her—a second thought all these years later? Yet every time she recalled those painful memories,

23

she felt defiled all over again. She was retaining his sins every day, and it was not punishing *him*—it was poisoning *her*. She had a toxic problem. To get the poison out of her system, she needed to get the unforgiveness out of her trunk. Forgiving her abuser might not erase her memories, but it would take the pain out of them. The poison would evaporate.

"I don't think I *can* forgive," she said again.

"Pray with me from your heart."

"Okay," she whispered, and I led her in prayer.

Denise forgave her abuser that day, and she agreed to pray for him every day that followed. It was the best thing she ever did. About two months later as I was preaching a sermon, I looked over and there she was, sitting close, and I mean *really* close, to her husband. Her arm was around him; his arm was around her. I watched them while I was preaching; they were so absorbed in each other that they could have passed for newlyweds. When I caught him leaning down and kissing her, I thought, *Hey, that's great, but wait till you get home!*

Wow! What happened to them? She got rid of yesterday and let go of all the junk that held her back. Then she reached ahead to grab hold of what God has for her today and tomorrow.

Are you feeling the sting of painful memories in your trunk? Are you poisoning yourself with unforgiveness? Maybe you have both hands full of yesterday, and you relive it every day. You cannot have great todays or tomorrows if you are still hoarding poisonous junk from yesterday. But if you will let go of the past and forgive, you will clean out those deadly toxins. Unload some of the junk from your trunk. Do as Paul said—forget what is behind and reach ahead to what God has for you.

The Spiritual Blinders of Pride

Aren't you glad that God forgives us? That is the best news anyone can ever hear! Remember the story about the time Jesus was preaching inside a house and four men brought their paralytic friend to see Him? Because of the crowd there was no way to enter the house, so those four guys climbed onto the roof—no simple task while carrying a paralytic—broke open a hole and lowered the man on his bed down to Jesus. Talk about interrupting a service! When I preached as a missionary, there would be children, dogs, chickens and even a pig in the service, but no one ever lowered a bed through the roof!

You would think that after all this man had suffered and all his friends had gone through, Jesus' first words would involve healing. Yet Matthew 9:2 tells us: "When Jesus saw their faith, He said to the paralytic, 'Son, . . . your sins are forgiven you.'" Jesus also said "take up your bed and walk," but that came second. He gave the paralytic the most important gift first—forgiveness.

But the lesson does not stop there. Many times we see forgiveness only as vertical, coming down from God, but He means forgiveness to be horizontal, too—we receive it and pass it on. No matter how someone else wronged you or me, it cannot compare with our sins against God. He forgives us, so we must forgive others. The Gospel requires it. When we think we are so important and the damage done to us is so great that we need not forgive, we make ourselves greater than God, who freely forgives all. To assume that we can store offense toward others side by side in our trunks with the forgiveness God grants us is a sign of pride.

With pride, wrote Solomon, comes "nothing but strife"; wisdom, on the other hand, is "with the well-advised" (Proverbs 13:10). We are wise to take counsel from God's Word and from godly advisors. If we choose not to, if we keep our own counsel and nurture the sin of pride, we strive against the Gospel. We pack spiritual blinders in our trunks—pieces of junk we definitely don't need! It is too tempting to put them on and deceive ourselves.

What might we be blinded to? Predominantly our relationship with God! I know people who take pride in thinking they have a great spiritual life. They say, "God and I are friends, *we're* walking hand in hand. But if you knew my spouse! My parents! My siblings! . . ." Their hearts are full of bitterness toward others, but they think they have a great walk with God. That is impossible! First John 4:20 addresses that attitude: "If someone says, 'I love God,' and hates his brother, he is a liar; for he who does not love his brother whom he has seen, how can he love God whom he has not seen?"

You cannot love God, whom you have not seen, if you cannot love relatives, friends and passersby whom you have seen. On any given Sunday in my city, there are probably fifty thousand people who stay home from church because they are offended. Someone at their church said or did something, or did not say or do something, and it hurt, so they are bitter. "I love God," they claim, "but I can't handle those church people. I'm better off worshiping God in my own way."

That is one self-deception that showed up early in history and has been showing up ever since. Cain and Abel were the first two people born on earth. Whether or not they were twins, as some Bible scholars believe, they certainly didn't "do church" the same way. God had already shown their family what was required as a response to His holiness. The innocent had to die for the guilty, and Adam's family knew it. When Adam and Eve sinned, God killed some animals and made tunics out of the skins to clothe them. (I believe the animals were sheep, because Jesus is called the Lamb of God.) But when Cain came to God with an offering, he did it his way. What did he bring? A bunch of vegetables. Abel brought what God had asked, a lamb out of the flock, and it pleased God.

One way we can see the spirit of the world, the spirit of the wicked one, at work is by observing how it urges people to set their own morality, to decide for themselves what is right and wrong, to approach God on their own terms, not His. Cain kept his own counsel about what to offer God, and the Bible says his works were evil. He disobeyed God, took offense at Abel and, in his unbridled bitterness, murdered his brother. Quite an indictment against the human race—of the first two people ever born, one murdered the other. Not good! Notice what 1 John 3 says about their situation:

> In this the children of God and the children of the devil are manifest: Whoever does not practice righteousness is not of God, nor is he who does not love his brother. For this is the message that you heard from the beginning, that we should love one another, not as Cain who was of the wicked one and murdered his brother. And why did he murder him? Because his works were evil and his brother's righteous.
>
> 1 John 3:10–12

The Bible says Cain was connected to the wicked one, the devil. He was prideful and self-deceived. He was wearing spiritual blinders. When we let bitterness into our lives, as Cain did, we become spiritually blind, and he who hates his brother is in darkness:

27

He who says he is in the light, and hates his brother, is in darkness. . . . He who hates his brother is in darkness and walks in darkness, and does not know where he is going, because the darkness has blinded his eyes.

1 John 2:9, 11

The worst type of deception is self-deception. With that kind of junk in your trunk, you will think you are doing right when you are doing wrong. You will justify yourself, but the Bible says you are blind.

The Danger of Fatal Connections

This time it was a wife whose husband needed "fixing." She told me how "Eric," as we will call him, had a drinking problem. "He's never home before two A.M. He's always at the bar," she told me. "It's destroying our marriage. Our kids are a mess. It's affecting all our family relationships. . . . What can we *do*?"

"Let's organize an intervention," I suggested, and explained to her how this type of confrontation works. "Alcoholics Anonymous recommends that you assemble a person's family and friends together to tell him how his drinking is affecting all their lives. Then they ask him to go for help."

"All right, we'll do it," she agreed.

I attended, and I remember it as if it were yesterday. Eric did not know about the session beforehand, so he was shocked by what he saw.

I was shocked by what he did *not* see.

First his wife told him her painful story. Then his kids began. They were in tears as they talked about how they felt afraid of him. Person after person followed with facts of how his drinking was affecting their lives. At the end, I asked Eric if he understood that he had a problem.

"I may have some little problem, but I'm *nothing* like my dad," he argued. "Now *he* was a so-and-so and he abused my mother and me. . . ."

He stormed on and on; his father was this, his father was that. He carried in his trunk all the junk his father had ever dumped on him, and it was blinding him to his own condition.

As I sat listening to him, I thought, *You've become just like your dad.*

When you do not forgive people, you become connected to them. You may become the exact opposite of them or, amazingly, blinded by your hate, you may become just like them.

Jesus said, "If you forgive the sins of any, they are forgiven them; if you retain the sins of any, they are retained" (John 20:23). One way you retain someone else's sins is in your mind. You stay connected to that person because you are constantly thinking about what he or she did to you. When you harbor bitterness against someone, that person and that person's sins will affect you the rest of your life.

Several years ago, a guest speaker at our church also illustrated this principle perfectly. The speaker, whom I'll call "Bill," told us an intriguing true story about his own near-fatal connection to a man he hated. Bill's father was a successful businessman involved in several different ventures. His life was cut short by murder. When the police investigated the homicide, they came up empty-handed. They informed Bill that all they could be sure about was that the murder had been a professional hit.

That was not enough for Bill. In response he dedicated the next several years of his life to acting as a private investigator. The top case on his list? His father's murder. He dug continually until he found evidence of who was behind the brutal act. Everything pointed toward one of his father's business associates, who thought that in order to secure a financial advantage, he had to have Bill's father assassinated. Bill found out who the hit man was, how he had been paid, and several other details vital to the case. He then presented all his evidence to the district attorney's office.

After examining the evidence closely, the DA looked at him and said, "There is no question that this man killed your father. However, your method of obtaining this evidence makes it inadmissible in court. We can't go to trial."

That was not enough for Bill. He told us how, disappointed and outraged, he came to a conclusion: *Since they won't give me justice, I'll take justice into my own hands.* He began to follow his father's murderer; he watched his every move. Once Bill understood the man's routine, he planned his revenge. He bought a 12-gauge shotgun (since buckshot cannot be traced) and picked his spot: an orchard about twenty miles outside town. Bill knew exactly how it would go: The man played poker at the same time and place every week. Bill would pick him up after a game. Then he would drive to the orchard and tie the man to a tree. He had memorized what he would say, and when he had had his say, he would kill him.

At last the day he had planned so carefully arrived. Bill told us, "That very day I was going to pick him up after his poker game and murder him. But God got hold of me and I got saved."

What really shocked our congregation as we listened to his story, though, was his next statement: "Because I did not forgive, I became what he was. He was a murderer, and in my heart, I became a murderer."

Because he could not let go of yesterday, bitterness had this man living one of the lowest lives imaginable, that of a murderer. Because of his unforgiveness, he was fatally connected to the man who had hurt him. Thoughts of revenge consumed his whole life. Had he taken his revenge, it likely would have cost him everything he had. God helped him find a better plan, and he let go of the offense. As the Italian proverb goes, "To forget a wrong is the best revenge."

"Going on with your life" means clearing the poison out of your system and letting go of painful yesterdays. *Forgiveness enables you to detoxify and reach out for your tomorrows.* Going on with your life depends upon releasing pride and self-deception. *Forgiveness removes your spiritual blinders.* Going on with your life requires breaking the fatal connections that keep you bound to people who have wronged you. *Forgiveness sets you free.*

I heard about a monkey hunter who caught monkeys by placing a banana inside a jug that was chained to a tree. The opening was just big enough for the monkey to reach in, but once he grabbed the banana he could not get it back out. Now the monkey could easily escape becoming someone's monkey stew if it would just *let go* of the banana, but he stubbornly clung to it—to his own destruction. Unless we *let go* of the hurtful events of our past we will not be free to escape and take hold of the freedom to enjoy life either. Without forgiveness we cannot put the past behind us. As we will discover more and more in the chapters ahead, forgiveness is the most important step we can take if we are serious about cleaning the junk out of our trunks.

31

Unloading Your Trunk

1. Is there anyone in particular you would like to poison? Not literally, of course, but someone you want to get what you think he or she deserves? That might indicate the presence of poison in your own trunk. You *can* let it go. Take some time to pray or even write out a short prayer of forgiveness, and begin to pray for that person daily. It may seem hard, but it is the best thing you can do for yourself.

2. Have you ever, like Cain, determined to set your own moral rules and come to God on your own terms? Invite God, as in Psalm 139:23–24, to search your heart and show you any wrong thinking that you may be unaware of.

3. Have you ever been told that you are a carbon copy of—or maybe the exact opposite of—someone who has negatively affected your life? If you feel that your life is bound in any way to that person, you have stored a fatal connection in your trunk. Sever it by forgiving him or her—by choosing on purpose to hold that person's wrongs against him or her no longer. Leave them for God to handle and free yourself.

— 3 —

A Trunk Full of
Torment and Trouble

The apostle Peter may have struggled with junk in his trunk, specifically unforgiveness. One day he asked Jesus, "Lord, how often shall my brother sin against me, and I forgive him? Up to seven times?" (Matthew 18:21). Peter believed that forgiving an offender seven times was generous indeed. He was probably thinking, *There's this guy doing the same thing to me over and over, and I'm offering to forgive him seven times! Isn't that amazing, Jesus?*

Peter expected a pat on the back, but Jesus replied, "I do not say to you, up to seven times, but up to seventy times seven" (verse 22). That would be *490 times.*

The spirit of Jesus' statement does not suggest you grab a legal pad and tally how many times you forgive, till you reach your limit. Sometimes you might reach the 490 mark! The spirit of it means that no matter how many times someone wrongs you, you keep on forgiving.

As further answer to Peter's question, Jesus told a parable about someone who kept a tally on his legal pad and refused to mark any offense as "forgiven."

A certain king wished to settle accounts with his servants. One owed him ten thousand talents—about twenty million dollars today—but could not pay. The king commanded that he, his wife, his children and all that he had be sold to pay the debt. The servant fell down before his master and cried, "Master, have patience with me, and I will pay you all" (verse 26). Not likely a servant could ever repay twenty million dollars! The master "was moved with compassion, released him, and forgave him the debt" (verse 27).

That servant soon ran across a fellow who owed him a hundred denarii—about a hundred days' wages, or six thousand to ten thousand dollars today. Now, he didn't politely call the fellow over and ask for the money as the king had done with him. He laid hands on him violently and took him by the throat, saying, "Pay me what you owe!" (verse 28). When the fellow pleaded for patience, he threw him in prison.

Other servants who witnessed the exchange were appalled and reported it to the king. Again the servant forgiven of the huge debt was summoned before his master. This time the outcome was not so pleasant. His master rebuked him: "You wicked servant! I forgave you all that debt because you begged me. Should you not also have had compassion on your fellow servant, just as I had pity on you?" (verses 32–33). Then he delivered the unforgiving servant to the torturers until he should pay all that was due! "So My heavenly Father also will do to you if each of you, from his heart, does not forgive his brother his trespasses," Jesus concluded (verse 35).

Notice a couple of things here: One man was forgiven a *huge* debt, then sought out his fellow servant who owed him about three months' wages. It was a substantial amount, but it was nothing like the debt he himself had been forgiven. Yet this man refused to forgive someone else. When his fellow servants saw it, the Bible says they were grieved. The master, upon hearing the news, addressed the man this way: "You wicked servant!" The servant was not called wicked because he had stolen money, committed adultery or murdered anyone. He had simply refused to forgive.

Sometimes you and I label certain sins as the worst ones possible. I believe that spiritual sins are the worst in God's sight, and that He sees unforgiveness as uglier than just about any other sin. If someone steals, there can be forgiveness. The same is true for adultery or murder. Remember, however, that in verse 35 of this parable, Jesus said that if we do not forgive others, neither will our Father in heaven forgive us. When we refuse to forgive, it grieves God more deeply than just about anything else we can do.

In the last chapter we noted the pride of trying to store unforgiveness toward others side by side in our trunks with the forgiveness God grants us. God expects that when we receive forgiveness, we pass it on. Because we have been forgiven, we should find it not only possible but easy to forgive one another. If we refuse, however, we learn from this story of the wicked servant that such arrogance leads to grave consequences.

Just as the master turned his wicked servant over to the torturers in the parable, the Father in heaven will turn us over to the torturers if we refuse to forgive. Who and what are the torturers? They are Satan and demonic powers. Unforgiveness specifically opens the door for them to attack our lives. Maybe our minds will be tormented by awful memories. Maybe our families will be tormented by our sinful habits. Maybe a passion for revenge will consume our every waking moment.

There will be no peace when there are torturers in your trunk. The best thing to do is close the door—and the lid of your trunk—on the torturers by forgiving others. When you forgive, you refuse to take torment along for the ride.

Rooting Out Trouble

Torment is not the only thing trying to ride in your trunk when you don't forgive. Trouble tags along, too, and it is like mold or mildew—the longer it goes untreated, the farther it spreads. Or think of it as a weed. If you pull up a sprouting weed by the roots as soon as you see that little thing, it is no big deal. You save yourself some trouble later. But if you wait . . . isn't it amazing how you don't need to fertilize weeds? You never need to plant or water them. All my grass can be dead and dying, I mean, *entirely* brown. And this weed will grow tall and green right in the middle of it!

The same thing happens with a root of bitterness. We will be talking about roots of bitterness in greater detail later, but for now recognize that resentment and unforgiveness are bitter roots. Where a root starts, growth starts, and then up springs a weed. If you choose to forgive rather than become offended, you are pulling out little roots of bitterness that have just sprouted. They are no big deal. But if you let them start to grow inside you, that is all the effort you need to make to ensure their rapid development. From that small beginning, the Bible says that roots spring up and cause trouble: "Looking carefully lest anyone fall short of the grace of God; lest any root of bitterness spring-

ing up cause trouble, and by this many become defiled"
(Hebrews 12:15).

Do you like to garden? Jeanie likes to garden, so I garden.
We work on it all the time. We plant tomatoes and peppers,
we plant squash and cauliflower, but the weeds, they just
come up by themselves! All summer long, I have to get out
there every week with the rototiller. I shake myself all over
up and down those rows, and I stop to pick all the weeds the
rototiller misses. If I let those little things get a head start,
that garden will be a mess—weeds everywhere—and I will
think, *That happened so fast! How did all those weeds get there?*
Simple: We were not diligent. We stopped pulling up weeds
when they were small. If we are not diligent, not "looking
carefully lest" any weeds spring up, pretty soon our garden
is in rough shape. It takes diligence to have a nice garden.

The Bible tells us we must employ the same kind of
diligence to have a clean heart. We have to stay on top of
it constantly and be careful about forgiving anything that
could cause us to take offense. If we are not looking at our
hearts carefully, diligently refusing to pick up offenses, then
bitterness roots itself deep inside us.

Remember: Wherever there is a root, there is a plant. It
might take a while, but the plant is going to pop up and it
is going to grow. Have you ever noticed how the part of a
weed that grows aboveground looks different from the part
that grows underground? Just so, your "visible" reactions to
bitterness may look quite different from the root of bitterness itself. You may gossip, you may lie, you may steal—no
one can predict the kind of weed that will sprout since
bitterness can make you do strange things. But whatever
you do because of bitterness, it will be ugly because it stems
from an ugly root. You cannot hold bitterness in your heart
and be free from trouble.

Some unforgiving people think, *I've got this against so-and-so, and it's going to hurt her!* It does not hurt her like it hurts you, though. Ninety percent of the people you hold resentment toward do not even know about it! They are living their lives and going their merry way, and you are thinking, *Hmm, they're supposed to be in pain over this—why am I the one feeling so miserable?* It is because you do not hurt them by allowing bitterness to grow; you hurt yourself.

You also hurt the people around you who are not even the target of your wrath. Hebrews 12:15 says that a root of bitterness causes trouble "and by this many become defiled." Remember the tearful pleas of Eric's wife and children in the last chapter and the effect his anger had on many other people? As we saw in that story, you start by defiling yourself, allowing bitterness to darken your conscience so that you become deceived. Add that condition, ugly enough by itself, to Ecclesiastes 7:9, which says, "Do not hasten in your spirit to be angry, for anger rests in the bosom of fools" and you have an equation that signals trouble. Anger residing inside you from unresolved conflicts will cause you to act foolishly and do things you otherwise would not do.

A bitter root plus anger plus foolishness equals trouble for you and everyone around you. Yet that is the situation we have today all over America. Literally millions of people are walking down the street or driving their cars with smiles on their faces, yet when you say or do something inconsequential to one of them, maybe by accident, he or she blows up: "Why, you . . . !" And you think, *What did I do? I sure made him mad!*

You did not do anything. People like that woke up mad. They went to bed last night mad. They woke up yesterday and the day before that mad. The truth is, they have been mad, some of them, for the last twenty years. Anger rests in

38

the bosom of fools—people who can smile on the outside, but just underneath the surface, all the time, they are waiting to explode. They believe someone mistreated them—and someone probably did. They believe what that person did to them was wrong—and it probably was. And they think, *I'm going to get him; he'll get what he deserves!*

Angry people really want recompense: They want those who hurt them to pay and they believe they can "blast" them with unforgiveness like a laser beam to get even. While light can be focused, anger can't. Focused light can produce tremendous energy. Think about what happens when the sun's power is focused. You women probably never did this. As a girl, you probably played with Barbie. But if you are a guy, did you take a magnifying glass outside when you were a kid, find an anthill and fry those ants? You smoked them! I thought so. I did, too. (We repent, Lord!) We took the power of the sun, which was shining down on those ants the whole time, and we focused it to produce that tremendous—and to the ants terrible—energy.

People believe that they can focus unforgiveness in the same way to cause their offenders terrible recompense. You and I need to understand that this will never happen. Anger resting in your bosom can never be focused. It always explodes like a hydrogen bomb, causing collateral damage all around you. You may be furious with your boss, but guess who gets burned? Your wife, your kids, your friends, your coworkers—everybody close to you, because a hydrogen bomb waits in your bosom. Sometimes you do not even know why you fly off the handle when others say or do the littlest thing. But the anger and resentment in your heart will not lie there dormant. You will explode!

In the *Translator's New Testament*, Hebrews 12:15 reads: "See to it that no one falls away from God's grace, that no bitterness springs up to cause trouble and *spoil everybody's life"* (italics added). When anger rests in your bosom, you spoil your own life and the lives of everyone around you.

Bitterness Builds a Gallows

When we spoil our lives and the lives of everyone close to us, it goes without saying that we will not know joy. As Christians, we ought not to look as if we are sucking lemons as we "endure to the end," but that is how life will seem without joy in our trunks. God did not give us life to endure. He wants us to enjoy life! He does not want us just to get to heaven. He wants us to enjoy the journey.

The book of Esther tells of a man, Haman, who had everything he could want to make life enjoyable:

> Then Haman told them [his wife and his friends] of his great riches, the multitude of his children, everything in which the king had promoted him, and how he had advanced him above the officials and servants of the king. Moreover Haman said, "Besides, Queen Esther invited no one but me to come in with the king to the banquet that she prepared; and tomorrow I am again invited by her, along with the king."
>
> Esther 5:11–12

Haman had it all. In today's economy, Haman would be a billionaire. As prime minister he commanded respect—the king's servants were under orders to bow down to him. Everything about his life was wonderful. He had wealth beyond our wildest dreams, fame, influence and a mansion with every toy available at that time. He even had a great family—*ten* sons! In the ancient world of the East, sons were *the* thing to have. If you had even five sons, you were nearly a king already in that culture!

I have three sons and a daughter, and I love them all. Sons are awesome, but they compete with you all your life! By the time they are two, they want to beat you up. They want to be faster, stronger, better than you! My daughter, she just loves me. That is one reason daughters are awesome, too—they just love you. But here was Haman with ten strong sons to keep him sharp, along with everything else the world had to offer. Yet he was miserable. Consumed with anger and revenge, he enjoyed none of it.

Haman hated Mordecai. Why? "When Haman saw that Mordecai did not bow or pay him homage, Haman was filled with wrath" (Esther 3:5). A huge root of bitterness took hold in Haman's heart, spoiling everything. After he listed all his possessions and privileges, he told his wife and friends, "Yet all this avails me nothing, so long as I see Mordecai the Jew sitting at the king's gate" (Esther 5:13).

What availed him nothing in the end, though, was his bitterness. Haman plotted to kill Mordecai, and not just Mordecai, but *all* the Jews as well. He built a gallows for Mordecai and laid plans to make sure all the Jews would pay terribly for the offenses he felt he had endured. The plot was discovered and brought to the attention of the king by Queen Esther herself. Haman was hanged on the very gallows he built for the man he resented. Soon afterward, Haman's ten sons were killed and hanged on that same gallows, their lives lost as a result of the hatred their father bore toward Mordecai.

Haman could not enjoy his life, and because of that, neither could those closest to him. His root of bitterness sprang up and defiled many. It poisoned many lives. It took many lives.

We cannot let bitterness grow, or we will not enjoy life anymore. We will not enjoy our families or friends or our careers or the benefits God has given us. We need to throw out every bit of bitterness *before* it puts out roots, springs up, and causes torment and trouble for us and for everyone around us.

Unloading Your Trunk

1. What limits have you reached lately? Have you made any statements like these? "That's the last time I'll put up with that." "He is really getting on my nerves." "I wouldn't give her the time of day if she were the last person on earth." What person and situation caused you to reach your limit? Pray for that person, and surrender your legal pad to the Lord. You won't need it anymore when you let Him direct the number of times you will forgive.

2. Is there anything that causes you mental anguish every time you think of it? What tortured memory or passion for revenge troubles your trunk? Search your heart for the unforgiveness that keeps opening the door of your mind to mental attack and anguish. If you refuse to carry your unforgiveness any farther, the torturers will have to find another ride as well.

3. Have you ever been around someone whose anger exploded like a bomb and burned everyone within earshot? That person's anger probably had a more focused target, but you were part of the collateral damage. Are you waiting to drop an anger bomb on someone? How might your anger be affecting the people closest to you who are not the target of your wrath? Stop the

collateral damage you are causing—do some spiritual weeding and forgive the person who offended you.

4. Can you recall a situation where you watched someone build his own gallows as Haman did, plotting and planning revenge on someone else only to have it backfire in the worst possible ways? Proverbs 5:22 warns, "His own iniquities entrap the wicked man, and he is caught in the cords of his sin." Can you recall a situation where you felt bitter toward someone and it was difficult for you to forgive, but you did it and avoided the trap of building your own gallows? How did that act of forgiveness increase your enjoyment of life and your peace? Can you think of other situations where forgiveness on your part would help you put joy back in your trunk?

4

Bury Me under
the Sycamine Tree

"I can't forgive—not yet." I have heard many people say this. They plan to forgive—eventually—but they have some excuse. They don't feel the person deserves it, or they think it will be easier later if they stew over it for a while first. Or they rationalize that they don't have to forgive until the person apologizes. In Mark 11:25, Jesus gave clear instructions as to when we should forgive:

> "And whenever you stand praying, if you have anything against anyone, forgive him, that your Father in heaven may also forgive you your trespasses."

He said *whenever* we pray we are to forgive. How often do you think Jesus anticipated that we should pray? Weekly? Monthly? On holidays? When Jesus taught the disciples to pray He said, "When you pray, say: . . . 'Give us each day our daily bread'" (Luke 11:2–3, NASB). That sounds as though it is at least a daily occurrence. And another time He said to "watch and pray so that you will not fall into temptation" (Matthew 26:41, NIV). I doubt there are any of us who can pass a day without some kind of temptation—to cheat, be impatient, gossip, be rude, lose our temper. . . . Jesus expects us to pray often, on a daily basis, and *whenever* we pray, we are to forgive.

"I can forgive most people, but not . . ." Jesus gave clear instructions about that, too. He said, "If you have *anything* against *anyone*." He didn't say that to be hard on us, but to make life better for us! Jesus expects us to forgive diligently—not just certain people sometimes, but everyone every time we pray—every day.

The consequences of not forgiving diligently are too great. Look at the following verse: "But if you do not forgive, neither will your Father in heaven forgive your trespasses" (Mark 11:26). Refusing to forgive others is *not* worth it!

We have explored several consequences of unforgiveness—how it opens the door to demonic torment, how "ugly" behavior grows out of bitterness, how our joy is destroyed. When we will not forgive others, we deny ourselves the gift of forgiveness. Nothing could be more terrible.

But we also lose something else: our ability to exercise our faith. In Mark 11:23–24, just ahead of those verses on forgiveness, Jesus gave the clearest, most concise teaching on faith that you will find anywhere in the Bible:

> "For assuredly, I say to you, whoever says to this mountain, 'Be removed and be cast into the sea,' and does not doubt in his heart, but believes that those things he says will be done, he will have whatever he says. Therefore I say to you,

whatever things you ask when you pray, believe that you receive them, and you will have them."

Then He seemed immediately to switch gears in verses 25–26 and talk about unforgiveness. Why did He address unforgiveness right after one of His most important teachings on faith? I think the reason is because unforgiveness is the number one hindrance to faith. Jesus did not really switch gears—faith will not function with unforgiveness in our hearts.

The disciples recognized this. In Luke 17, as soon as Jesus told them they must forgive even seven times, they made an immediate request: "Increase our faith" (verse 5). Forgiveness is not a feeling, it is a decision. They knew they had to forgive by faith.

We usually think of Jesus' reply to their request as another of His most important teachings on faith—and so it is—but let's look at what else He was saying in verse 6: "If ye had faith as a grain of mustard seed, ye might say unto this sycamine tree, Be thou plucked up by the root, and be thou planted in the sea; and it should obey you" (KJV).

Notice Jesus mentioned a sycamine tree, which I believe He chose as His illustration because of its characteristics. Although Jesus was talking about faith, the sycamine tree's characteristics make it a perfect illustration of forgiveness—or the lack thereof.

We will look more closely at the sycamine tree's characteristics—its growth rate, the use of its wood, its preferred climate, its root system development, the fruit it produces and its method of pollination—in the rest of this chapter. But to start, think of the sycamine tree as an offense that you need to forgive. If you say to that offense, "be thou plucked up *by the root*, and be thou planted in the sea" (italics added), you have taken a bitter root and cast it into the sea of forgiveness before it could take hold and cause you any serious trouble. You have forgiven your brother *and* kept from harboring bitter junk in your trunk. Likewise, your heavenly Father will forgive you, casting your sins into the sea of forgetfulness and no longer holding them against you.

Now suppose that sycamine tree represents an offense that you refuse to forgive. This time the sycamine tree's characteristics illustrate what happens when you let a bitter root take hold. They are a warning against cultivating unforgiveness.

Growing Your Own Coffin

The sycamine tree grows quickly. For this reason, its wood was the most preferred wood in Egypt and the Middle East for building coffins. I think Jesus used the sycamine as an example of unforgiveness for the same reason, because of its quick growth rate. We need to recognize that a bitter root grows quickly, just as the sycamine tree does. We must not give bitterness one single day to grow!

Ephesians 4:26–27 warns, "'Be angry, and do not sin': do not let the sun go down on your wrath, nor give place to the devil." If we let the sun go down, if we let just *one day* pass, we give Satan a foothold. In 1 Samuel 18, the Israelites were coming back from the victory over the Philistines. David had killed Goliath, and Saul became jealous of David because the women greeted the army by singing, "Saul has slain his thousands, and David his ten thousands" (verse 7). Saul picked up offense at that and "eyed David from that day forward" (verse 9). Saul did not root out his resentment immediately, and notice Scripture says that on the very next day an evil spirit came upon Saul (verse 10). It only took *one day*!

Besides growing quickly, the sycamine tree will grow in any environment. The same goes for a bitter root. It does not matter whether you are illiterate or have two Ph.D.s. Your social level, your ethnic background and your family life do not matter either. Bitterness will grow in any person at any age in any country, and its effects are absolutely devastating.

Interestingly, the *preferred* climate of the sycamine is a dry climate. That is doubly true when it comes to bitterness growing in your life. The drier you are spiritually and the farther you are away from God, the more likely you are to let bitterness grow. When you are not seeking God, not worshiping, not in church, not repenting, not in joy, not praying and not forgiving others from your heart every day—when you are dry spiritually—bitterness will grow even faster. It sets up a continuous cycle that will put you under: The faster bitterness grows, the drier you become spiritually, and the drier you become spiritually, the faster bitterness grows.

In his book *When Life Throws You a Curve* (Albury Publishers, 1998), Billy Joe Daugherty makes this fascinating observation: "Rarely does a young person go into immorality, drugs, or alcohol who does not have bitterness in his or her heart. Why? Because bitterness is like AIDS. While AIDS breaks down the physical immune system, bitterness breaks down the spiritual immune system."

If you contract AIDS, unless God intervenes, sooner or later you will die. It is a virus, and it is difficult—if not impossible—to cure a virus. It is much better not to contract the virus in the first place. Likewise, bitterness is a spiritual virus and it will destroy your spiritual immune system. If you pick up bitterness, unless you forgive by faith and let God work in your heart, sooner or later it will kill you spiritually. Just as they used to take that fast-growing sycamine wood and build a coffin in which to bury someone, a fast-growing root of bitterness—spiritual AIDS—will provide all that is needed to bury you spiritually. It won't take very long, either.

Returning to Your Roots

The root structure of the sycamine tree is very large and goes very deep, which makes it hard to kill. You can chop down a sycamine tree, cart away all the wood and return a year or two later to find that the stump you left in the ground is literally growing rampant. The sycamine tree almost always comes back—unless you get rid of the root.

Perhaps Jesus had that in mind when He talked about bearing good fruit: "And even now the ax is laid to the root of the trees. Therefore every tree which does not bear good fruit is cut down and thrown into the fire" (Luke 3:9). If you have let bitterness grow, laying the ax to the root of your unforgiveness may involve more than one step. Have you ever admitted, "I thought I forgave him, but when I saw him six months later, I wanted to shoot him!"? Or "I thought I took care of this! I can't believe the resentment that rose up inside at the sight of her"? What happened? You forgave by faith, but your feelings did not follow your faith. Resentment was still riding in your trunk.

But you can lay the ax to the root and be free from those feelings, too. It's a matter of staying with it until you see it through.

Now, that may sound like "work," but using the right tools can make all the difference! Last summer I took out a stump for Jeanie. I knew my job would be much easier if I used the right tool, a sharp ax. I also knew that one swing of the ax would not do it. I made that first swing count—the ax bit deeply through one root—but that strike was not sufficient by itself to remove the stump. Because I had the right tool, though, each succeeding strike was effective. I stayed with it until each root was severed and that stubborn stump no longer had any connection to keep it in the ground. Before long I was showing my wife a beautiful clearing where that stubborn stump had once hung on.

Forgiving by faith is the initial step you take in your heart—it is like that first swing of the ax—but it is not the final step. Faith without works is dead. When you receive the Lord by faith, you walk it out every day. You work at it. The same thing is true in forgiving someone. You make a decision to forgive by faith, but you still need to do something: You need to see it through by putting works with your faith. Some works are beneficial—they are the right tools—and some are not. Let's take a look.

Accosting Your Offender

Sometimes when people forgive, they try to add works that just do not . . . work. They think they need to clean their slates by accosting their offenders with all the details: "You did such-and-such, and I could have strangled you! Now I'm forgiving you." Often the offender has no clue what he did, so the encounter completely blows him away.

I got blown away like that when we were down in Guadalajara, Mexico. I was teaching in a Bible school, and my teachings on faith and healing were very different from what had been taught there before. I admit I rocked a few religious boats and kicked a few sacred cows, though I did not realize at the time how much shaking I was causing.

In one service, a visiting preacher told us that if we had anything against anyone, we should get up immediately and go tell that person. I was standing up front, and before I could blink, I had a line of about twenty people in front of me all waiting to tell me how I had offended them. The first person started right in: "I don't agree with what you think the Bible says about such-and-such. I'm so mad! But I forgive you." Then the next in line followed, and on it went. I had no clue that I had offended anyone like that. I thought I was simply preaching the Word. It blew me away, all right. That is not the kind of work faith does when it forgives.

Matthew 18:15 directs us to talk with those who have offended us, but the motivation must be love—regaining a brother or sister. It does not say that you are supposed to dump all your anger, hurt or misunderstanding on someone you picked up offense from! You may find, in fact, that you are able to settle the matter in your heart and gain the Lord's peace without approaching the person at all. You must seek the Lord's guidance and act only as He directs you.

Then the Bible says further that if you remember your brother has something *against you*, leave your gift at the altar and go to him and be reconciled (see Matthew 5:23–24). In other words, *if someone has offended you*, approach that brother or sister in love in order to be reconciled. *If you have offended someone*, approach him or her in love as well, so that the offense may be cleared. Remember to treat the person—particularly the one who has offended you—as you would like to be treated.

Praying for Your Offender

So what is the work you should engage in? When you forgive by faith, you add the work of exerting the time and energy to pray for your offender.

Now you may wonder, *Can I pray that he has an accident? Can I pray that he goes bankrupt? How about a tornado hitting his house?* In a word, no. Pray the blessing of God on his life. Pray for God's will to be done in him. Pray that God will give him the spirit of wisdom and revelation in the knowledge of Him (see Ephesians 1:17). If the person is not saved, pray that God will send laborers into his life, grant him repentance and open his heart to the Gospel. Bind the devil, in Jesus' name, from blinding his eyes. Pray for him each day, every day and speak well of him. Cover his sin by keeping it to yourself, not broadcasting it. How long must you work at forgiveness? Until all your resentful feelings are gone.

Something supernatural happens in such prayer. When you pray to God, your heart turns toward God. When you pray for someone you forgave, your heart turns toward that person. Romans 5:5 says "the love of God has been poured out in our hearts by the Holy Spirit." You keep praying for that person, and the love poured out in your heart by the Holy Spirit begins to rise up. It might take three days, three weeks or three years, but suddenly when you see that person, you feel compassion and love, not resentment and anger. A miracle of healing restoration has taken place inside you! You can rejoice over good things happening for that person. You are free from the caustic effects of unforgiveness! If any resentful feelings return, just start praying again. Every time you do, you lay the ax to any root of bitterness.

Do you see how vital it is to walk out the forgiveness that you offer by faith? Do not just forgive by faith. Start *blessing* your offenders by faith and praying for them by faith. It takes more time and energy to get rid of the sycamine tree's root system than it does to chop down the tree itself, but the end result is a nice clearing where the sycamine once grew. Likewise it takes more work to pull up a root of bitterness you have allowed to grow than it does to forgive an offense right away, but you can do it. And the end result is a nice clearing in your heart where bitterness once grew rampant.

The Sting of Bitter Fruit

The fruit of the sycamine tree looks like the fruit of a fig tree. If you have never had figs right off a fig tree, you have missed half your life! Take a fresh fig right off the tree, crack it open and there is nothing else like it—incredible!

Sycamine fruit looks like a fig, but when you eat it you will want to spit it out fast. Poor people actually bought sycamine fruit as a substitute for figs in biblical times, but they could not eat and enjoy the fruit as if it were a fig. They had to eat only a little bite at a time because it was so bitter.

If you start eating the fruit of your bitterness, you will not enjoy it either. It will bankrupt you spiritually and you will end up buying into substitutes—a curse instead of a blessing, depression instead of joy, strife instead of peace, a victim mentality instead of a positive attitude, dead faith instead of living, working faith. Sycamine fruit instead of figs.

At least you will have some company in your misery— the wasps will gather around you. Wasps are vital to the sycamine tree's reproduction. They pollinate the tree; a sycamine is unable to reproduce without their help. A wasp must stick its stinger into the heart of the sycamine fruit to initiate pollination. I think that such a wasp is a type of the devil. If you produce the bitter fruit of un-forgiveness, the devil and his demonic hordes will gather around to sting it. Then, just as the wasp penetrates deep into the middle of the sycamine fruit with its stinger, the devil penetrates deep into your life with his sting. He may attack your finances. He may attack your family or your health. He may attack your mind or your emotions. He stings you in multiple places. And your offender doesn't even feel the pain. You do.

Anyone and Anything

Satan would like to build a coffin in which to bury your spiritual life, and he will do it if you let a bitter root of unforgiveness stay inside your trunk. It is like handing him lumber and nails. He is, in fact, looking for you to supply the materials: a bitter root that has grown fast and deep, a poverty of spirit that keeps you bankrupt so you do not resist, some bitter fruit that he can put his stinger into so it reproduces. That is why it is so important, whenever you stand praying, to be diligent about using your faith to forgive anyone of anything you hold against him or her. Then continue to walk that forgiveness out in prayer.

Jesus used those two all-inclusive words, *anyone* and *anything*, in Mark 11:25: "And whenever you stand praying, if you have anything against anyone, forgive him." What does *anything* mean? Did he really mean *anything*, no matter what it is? What if someone lied about you, criticized you? Cut you off on the expressway! Is that included in *anything*? What about verbal, physical or even sexual abuse?

Anything.

Well, what about the word *anyone*? Did he really mean *anyone*, no matter who it is? When a salesclerk you have never met before is rude, you can forgive fairly easily. But what if your father abused you? Is he included in that *anyone*, too? Your wife left you for someone else. Is she in *anyone*? Anyone.

It does not matter who did it or what it was; Jesus said that you and I, while we stand praying, can forgive. Praying may only take five minutes. You can forgive by faith in five minutes. Then you do the work of walking it out in prayer.

Forgiveness does not mean that the evil someone did to you was right. And it does not mean that you should stay in a life-threatening situation in the name of forgiveness. Not at all! Get help for yourself and those you care for immediately if you are in danger of physical, mental or emotional abuse. Our point here is that once you know how much God has forgiven you, you learn to walk in the freedom of forgiving others and releasing them. You demand no recompense for what they did. You pray, *Lord, bless them.*

When we forgive, *we* get set free. Somehow we have the idea that when we forgive, we are doing something great for the person we are forgiving. And we *are* doing something for others when we forgive them. But really, forgiving others is the best thing we can do for ourselves. We can forgive anyone of anything while we stand praying, and when we do, we open the lid of our trunks and take out the bitterness. We also lay the ax to those building materials Satan wants to harvest for our spiritual coffins. We get them out of his hands and out of our trunks, and we leave a nice clearing in our hearts that we can fill with treasures like peace.

Unloading Your Trunk

1. What kind of climate are you growing your spiritual fruit in? Are you "like a tree planted by the riv-

ers of water, that brings forth its fruit in its season"
(Psalm 1:3), or are you in a dry place, feeling more like
a sycamine tree heavy with bitter fruit and stinging
wasps? Maybe you feel fruitless, already dead inside.
If Satan has buried you spiritually using a coffin of
your own making, that doesn't have to be the end of it!
Jesus rose from the grave, and He will raise you, too.
Abandon your dry climate by crying out to Him for
help. Then lay the ax to any bitter roots by forgiving
those who offended you, no matter who they were or
what they did. That way, you will crush the stinging
wasp beneath your feet.

2. Have you made the effort to forgive someone by faith,
only to find that your resentment keeps returning?
Maybe you pulled the weed of unforgiveness that
sprouted on the surface, but you missed its deeper
root system. Now your bitterness keeps returning to
its roots and growing back. Clear your trunk of lingering resentment by putting works with your faith:
No matter how long it takes, pray for your offender
daily until all your resentful feelings are gone.

3. Research shows it takes 21 days to form a habit. Make
yourself a reminder note that reads: "Do I have *anything* against *anyone* today? Do I need to uproot any
unforgiveness from my heart? Have I prayed for the
people I found hardest to forgive? Lord, forgive me
as I have forgiven others today." Hang the note where
you will see it every day for the next 21 days. "And
whenever" you pray, consider your reminder note. Soon
weeding out bitter roots will become a daily habit
for you.

5

The Mind-Numbing
Effects of Bitterness

When you look at life through hurt and anger, you are blinded to what is truly important. Bitterness keeps you focused on "issues" that irritate you, and as a result, you cannot see your situation clearly. You are left with a false picture of reality. The effects are mind-numbing.

My wife, Jeanie, has an ancestor who displayed a typical side effect—loss of good judgment. It is quite a story of the mind-numbing—and deadly—effects of bitterness.

Bitterness Causes Loss of Judgment

Everardus Bogardus (yes, that was his real name) was very involved in the early history of New York City, originally the pioneer Dutch colony called New Netherland. In April 1633, he arrived to pastor the congregation there. From some of the historical (and hysterical!) accounts we have read, he must have been a spunky, in-your-face character. Everywhere he went, the feathers flew in all directions as he confronted individuals both within his congregation and throughout the settlement. He also expressed himself freely and frequently against the exploitation of the Indians, unfair profiteering, covetousness and other excesses in the colony's government. I think he could have used Dale Carnegie's course called "How to Win Friends and Influence People," or else he needed to more fully realize the truth of Proverbs 15:1: "A soft answer turns away wrath, but a harsh word stirs up anger."

What Bogardus lacked in tactfulness, however, he made up for in zeal. He harshly denounced New Netherland's Director General, William Kieft, from the pulpit for misgoverning the colony. Kieft and his abettors were driven from the church. In reprisal, Kieft had drums beaten and cannon discharged outside the church while Bogardus was preaching! Kieft also accused the minister of dishonoring the pulpit and summoned him to court for inciting riot and rebellion.

The ill feelings, retaliation and gossip caused by their differences kept these two men busy loading their "trunks" with plenty of junk during their stay in New Netherland. Eventually they boarded the same ship bound for Holland, and their antagonism continued on board. Sources suggest that Bogardus undertook the dangerous passage mainly to lay his case against Kieft before a high official back in the fatherland. Kieft was allegedly returning home with a fortune in ill-gotten gains, which he had extracted from the settlement. Their bitterness drew them away from family and loved ones, and grew until they were consumed by it—literally. Both men perished when the ship sank off the coast of Wales.

Bitterness does not sit idle. It grows until it overshadows your life. Its mind-numbing side effects can cost you your good judgment. These men struggled to the last to prove each other wrong, but they never even made their day in court. Bitterness is deadly.

Bitterness Undermines Genius and Position

Absalom and Ahithophel were two others who gave their lives to bitterness and suffered its mind-numbing effects, in this case, loss of genius and position.

Absalom was one of King David's sons, and he tried to overthrow his father's throne. What caused his rebellion? Bitterness toward David. Absalom's beautiful sister, Tamar, had been raped by another half brother, Amnon. Although their father, David, heard about it and was furious, he did nothing to punish Amnon. David's refusal to deal with that situation at home greatly provoked Absalom, who took matters into his own hands and killed Amnon two years later. He justified his actions with thoughts of Tamar. Amnon was not the only target of his bitterness, though. Absalom also planned to kill David.

Ahithophel was counselor to King David and also let his hatred toward him grow. Second Samuel 16:23 says this: "Now the advice of Ahithophel, which he gave in those days, was as if one had inquired at the oracle of God." He was brilliant. His counsel was so wise it was as if God Himself had spoken. Despite his brilliance, though, he shared something deadly with Absalom. Like spirits attract: Both men were full of bitter hatred toward David.

What happened in Ahithophel's case? Ahithophel's granddaughter was Bathsheba (see 2 Samuel 11:3; 23:34). His bitter reaction to her difficult circumstances showed she was the apple of his eye. You probably know her story. She married Uriah, one of the top thirty officers in David's army, and she lived right next to the palace. Her grandfather must have been bursting with pride. One evening from his rooftop, King David saw Bathsheba bathing and took a wrong turn in his mind. He inquired about her and sent for her, a decision that led to adultery. She became pregnant with the king's child.

Try as he might, David could not get Bathsheba's husband to go home to her so that the world could think the child was a result of their reunion. Uriah was too honorable a leader to enjoy, even for one night, what his men in the battlefield could not. He paid for his honor with his life. Since David could not hide the sin under the cover of Uriah's visit, he sinned yet more by sending orders to the battlefront with Uriah: "Set Uriah in the forefront of the hottest battle, and retreat from him, that he may be struck down and die" (2 Samuel 11:15). Commander Joab followed orders, and Uriah died.

David had done grievous things, yet he repented, turning back to God for mercy and forgiveness. Grandfather Ahithophel was enraged and refused to forgive David. Remember, the Bible says bitterness is a root. Time does not heal it—over time that root grows. A decade passed, and Ahithophel's bitterness grew.

Ahithophel had been known as a wise man who gave flawless advice, but his judgment showed the wear and tear of years of bitterness. When Absalom rebelled against David, the anointed king, Ahithophel rebelled alongside him. Rebellion is one of the worst companions of bitterness (we will come back to that in the next chapter). When Absalom asked for advice, the counselor responded,

"Now let me choose twelve thousand men, and I will arise and pursue David tonight. I will come upon him while he is weary and weak, and make him afraid. And all the people who are with him will flee, and I will strike only the king. Then I will bring back all the people to you."

2 Samuel 17:1–3

That sounded grand to Absalom, but for one problem: Ahithophel had never strapped on a sword in his life! He had been counselor, not soldier. But how he longed to bring about David's downfall! "Let *me* choose," he advised. "*I* will arise. . . . *I* will strike. . . ." *I, I, I*—bitterness makes people think everything revolves around them and their frustrations.

Still, the Bible says that Ahithophel had given wise counsel for their evil plan, so the Lord caused Absalom and his men to discount it (see 2 Samuel 17:14). The rebels accepted the advice of another counselor and lost the battle. In the meantime, Absalom, amazingly, got his head caught in a great terebinth tree. His mule ran out from under him and left him "hanging between heaven and earth" (2 Samuel 18:9). Bitterness can leave you hanging in some dangerous positions! Commander Joab and his men found Absalom in that inglorious position and killed him.

Ahithophel, now disgusted with both Absalom and David, was left hanging by his bitterness, too: "When Ahithophel saw that his advice was not followed, he . . . put his household in order, and hanged himself, and died" (2 Samuel 17:23).

Counsel—even counsel as genius as if it were God's own—availed Ahithophel nothing against his deadly bitterness. Absalom's position as son of a mighty king did not save him from lethal consequences either. Bitterness undermines genius and position every time.

Bitterness Makes You "Dumb Yourself Down"

Smart people who become bitter fall under the mind-numbing effect of bitterness and do foolish things. I don't care if you have sixteen Ph.D.s or if the letters behind your name look like alphabet soup. If you put bitterness in your trunk, stupidity will jump in right behind it. Imagine putting on dark glasses that distort everything. Glasses tinted by bitterness cause you to see twisted images and misjudge your next move.

I have seen this happen time and again in marriages. Your spouse does something you do not forgive. It may be just a little thing, but that little seed springs up and soon bitterness distorts your spouse's image in your eyes. You start seeing your spouse through tinted glasses, and you stop thinking about the hundred wonderful things that caused you to fall in love. Your heart becomes hard, and walls go up that destroy the relationship. You cannot see through walls, so you lose sight of the treasure. Soon you entertain thoughts of separation and divorce.

Jesus told the Pharisees, "Moses, because of the hardness of your hearts, permitted you to divorce ... but from the beginning it was not so" (Matthew 19:8). At least one hard heart is involved in every divorce, but right from the start divorce was not in God's plan.

Consider this before "dumbing yourself down" with bitterness and making a foolish move: There are no perfect relationships because there are no perfect people. Everyone around you will someday say or do something wrong. Maybe he forgets your anniversary—again. Maybe she slides the car into the side of the garage—again. That happened to us one winter when we lived in a house on a hill. Icy conditions made putting the car away difficult. After several attempts to get the car into the garage one day, Jeanie backed way down the driveway for a "running start." She made it up the incline just fine, but then the car slid into the side of the garage. I was forgiving and had everything repaired. The next time there was ice on the driveway, though, she did the same thing with the same car in the same way—again. We made repairs—again (and later bought a house with a level driveway).

It almost seemed as though Jeanie did not "deserve" to be forgiven the second time—at least not so quickly! But if I had held anger toward her and allowed bitterness to twist my perception of her, soon everything about our marriage could have been tainted. Bitterness can start over a minor incident or two, but it quickly taints your whole marriage.

It doesn't matter whom you are married to, you can live a hundred years with him or her and love it. You can fall in love with your spouse a thousand times if you will forgive. "Be kind to one another, tenderhearted, forgiving one another, even as God in Christ forgave you," says Ephesians 4:32. A tender heart is merciful. Notice the last part of the verse tells us to forgive as God does. He removes our sins as far from us as the east is from the west. "I will forgive their iniquity, and their sin I will remember no more," God says in Jeremiah 31:34. Corrie ten Boom once added that then our sins are "cast into the deepest sea and a sign is put up that says, NO FISHING ALLOWED." I like that.

One man came to his pastor and said, "Pastor, every time my wife and I argue, she gets historical."

"Don't you mean she gets hysterical?" corrected the pastor.

"No, I mean she gets *historical*. She remembers everything I've done wrong for the past twenty years!"

If you get historical with your spouse and will not forgive, one of two things will happen: You will endure a rotten, unhappy marriage, or you will wind up downtown in divorce court. Those are your only options. When I see marriages end this way, I shake my head and think, *What's wrong with those people? Don't they see they had a brand-new Lamborghini in the garage and they gave it away for a used Volkswagen?*

To sacrifice an important relationship on the altar of your hard heart is a sure sign of dumbing yourself down with bitterness. Play it smart instead—take the bitterness out of your trunk and soften your heart toward God's command to forgive.

The Most Important Relationship of All

This is not just true in the relationship of marriage, of course. The mind-numbing effects of bitterness taint every relationship we have. Even our most important one.

Judas Iscariot sacrificed his most important relationship on the altar of his hard heart. He was Jesus' treasurer in charge of the money purse, and he kept a close watch on those purse strings!

Mark 14 tells us that Jesus and the disciples were at the house of Simon the Leper in Bethany. In came a woman carrying an alabaster flask of costly oil of spikenard. She broke it and poured *all* the oil on Jesus' head. Some of the disciples, particularly Judas Iscariot, were indignant. They asked, "Why was this fragrant oil wasted? For it might have been sold for more than three hundred denarii and given to the poor" (verses 4–5). They criticized her sharply for "wasting" more than three hundred days' wages (probably between $30,000 and $50,000 today).

Jesus rebuked them sharply: "Why do you trouble her? . . . You have the poor with you always, . . . but Me you do not have always. She has done what she could. She has come beforehand to anoint My body for burial" (verses 6–8). He promised that wherever the Gospel is preached, her act will be told as a memorial.

"Then Judas Iscariot," Scripture says, "went to the chief priests to betray Him" (verse 10). Why would Judas betray Him immediately after the scene at Bethany? I believe one reason was that Judas picked up offense at Jesus' public rebuke. Besides, Judas had other junk to deal with in his trunk. Scripture tells us he rebuked the woman not because he cared for the poor, "but because he was a thief, and had the money box; and he used to take what was put in it" (John 12:6). The junk Judas carried affected his most important relationship of all—his relationship with his Lord. His bitterness distorted his picture of Jesus, and Judas made his worst mistake—betraying the Messiah.

Unloading Your Trunk

1. Have you ever lost your good judgment and done something you now regret because your vision was impaired by bitterness? What would you do differently if faced with that situation again? Some things cannot be undone—Bogardus and Kieft lost their lives to bitterness. So did Absalom and Ahithophel. But it is not too late for you. Is there anything you can still do to redeem your poor decision? At the least, forgive

those who wronged you and pray for those whom you hurt with your actions.

2. If you are unhappily married, be honest about what part your perceptions play in your relationship. Review mentally the last half dozen thoughts you had about your spouse. Did they include anything positive? If not, maybe you need a "checkup from the neck up." Unless you forgive, you are in danger of divorce due to hardheartedness. Bitterness never gets better when left unattended, but it does grow bigger! Do not wait another day to educate yourself about strengthening your marriage. Many excellent Christian counselors and resources are available. God never intended you to pack the pain of a divorce in your trunk.

3. What is the condition of *your* most important relationship of all? Are you like the woman who gladly poured all the oil she had on her Lord? Or are you holding back because you are hurt and carrying the heaviest junk of all in your trunk—bitterness toward God? If so, chapter 10 will be especially important for you to read. I pray it will help you see a clearer picture of Him so that you can avoid sacrificing any part of your relationship with your Lord.

6

Bitterness Attracts Bad Company

As we have seen, bitterness in your trunk begets in you a false picture of reality and a tendency to do foolish things. Its effects on you do not stop there, however. Bitterness really is like that fast-growing sycamine tree we examined in chapter 4 that produces loads of bitter fruit. You nurture a small seed of offense, and before you know it, your trunk is full of all kinds of junk. Bitterness attracts bad company.

Bitterness is never alone. It invites a whole host of companions to join it in your trunk. Let's expose some of its worst companions and make sure they are not occupying our trunks.

A Complaining Spirit

One unhappy companion of bitterness is a complaining spirit. You may not realize it, but bitterness turns you into a whiner. Job commented in Job 7:11, "I will complain in the bitterness of my soul." When people complain and whine, I believe that much of the time their behavior results from bitterness. In the same verse, Job said, "I will not restrain my mouth." If you know any whiners, that probably applies to them. Whining becomes a continual habit for many people.

I knew a man who worked for one of the best employers in our city. One day he informed me, "I'm quitting my job so I can work for another company."

I was not surprised. Almost anyone would have been thrilled with his job, but he had complained about it constantly. One day he would say, "They give us too much overtime!" The next day he would say, "They give us too little overtime!" Another day he would say, "They make us start too early," then, "They make us stay too late." I also heard, "I have to park and walk too far to the building," and "My bonus is down and the boss bought a new car!" (If I had been his boss, I might have cut his bonus, too, based on attitude alone.) No matter what benefits he received, he was just not happy.

This man had much to be thankful for, but he had a distorted picture of his work situation and he was about to do something foolish. I thought, *In six months, you'll be just as upset with your new company and just as full of poison toward them.* When he changed jobs, I discovered I was wrong. It took fewer than six months before he started his complaints!

Sometimes we need a "checkup from the neck up" for hardening of the attitudes. Bitterness is an "anti" attitude—it is a hardening of your heart. Complaining, griping and nagging will flow from a heart becoming hardened by bitterness.

Emotional Exhaustion

Have you ever dealt with depression? If so, you are in the majority. Statistics show that 70 percent of Americans deal with depression, and that at any given time 30 percent are clinically depressed. Interestingly, one clinical definition of depression is "anger turned inward." Anger is resentment we hold on the inside. You think you are going to focus your anger in a certain direction, as we talked about in chapter 3, but instead it turns inward. Remember, "anger rests in the bosom of fools" (Ecclesiastes 7:9). From there it affects your emotional life.

If you harbor anger in your heart, you are using your emotional energy in the wrong place, and it will depress you. You only have so much energy available. Physically, you can only do a certain number of things before you feel worn out, then you need to rest and reenergize.

The same thing is true emotionally. You only have so much emotional energy. You can use it constructively to love, to support, to help, to persist in doing good. Then your emotions need to rest. When you hold on to bitterness, however, you quickly exhaust yourself. Bitterness is a tense, draining emotion that stays with you 24/7. Even in your "rest times" it constantly drains you, using huge amounts of your limited supply of emotional energy. You stop making progress in other areas of your life because bitterness robs you of enthusiasm, creativity and the ability to invest in relationships the way you should. It can leave you too depressed to function.

Have you ever stared at the ceiling late into the night, unable to sleep because someone hurt or frustrated you? You need sleep badly, but sleep is impossible. You cannot put your mind at rest because you keep going over and over the offense; you do not let go and forgive. No wonder you wake up depressed the next day—you are both physically and emotionally exhausted, and you have to get up and face others in that 70 percent who are dealing on and off with depression. . . .

Take yourself out of the majority by taking bitterness out of your trunk. Find relief from the emotional exhaustion bitterness produces and enjoy peaceful, refreshing nights of sleep!

A Taste for Strife and Gossip

"Six things the LORD hates, yes, seven are an abomination to Him," states Proverbs 6:16. Sowing strife among brothers makes that list. This companion of bitterness is so unwholesome that God considers it an abomination! When you gossip about an offense committed against you or someone else, you are welcoming strife into your trunk. You are also urging others to pack that offense into their trunks.

Certainly it is sometimes necessary to report an offense to someone in authority. In 1 Corinthians 5:1, Paul mentions that members of Chloe's household reported a case of sexual immorality. They were right to bring it to Paul. He had authority to handle it, helping or disciplining those involved and bringing healing to the situation. On the other hand, however, when you tell your friends how someone hurt you, how miserable you felt, how awful he or she was, that is not reporting. That is gossiping. You transfer the offense to your friends. The next week, you reconcile with your offender and have coffee together, but your friends are left out of the healing process. They are still angry over what you suffered. You have spread strife among brothers.

"Where envying and strife is, there is confusion and every evil work" (James 3:16, KJV). Your trunk will overflow with junk when you allow strife and gossip inside.

A Passion for Revenge

A vengeful spirit is another miserable companion of bitterness. Bitter people often display a passion for revenge. They are quick to judge others, particularly those who have offended them. Two disciples demonstrated a vengeful spirit in Luke 9. Jesus sent messengers ahead to a Samaritan village, to prepare for Him. The village did not receive Him because His face was set toward Jerusalem (see verses 52–53). When James and John saw this, their immediate response was, "Lord, do You want us to command fire to come down from heaven and consume them, just as Elijah did?" (verse 54).

Tremendous prejudice existed between the Jews and the Samaritans. The Samaritans were the remnant of the ten tribes that had separated from Judah; the Jews descended from the two tribes that had stayed faithful to the House of David. The Jews actually called the Samaritans dogs, but Jesus loved Samaritans and ministered to them. The woman at the well was a Samaritan. In this incident, however, the Samaritan village would not receive Him (vengeance continued on their side as well), so James and John wanted them punished. Because of longstanding bitterness toward the Samaritans, the disciples quickly displayed a passion for revenge.

When we thirst for revenge and want destructive things to happen in someone's life, we are operating in the wrong spirit. If we inwardly wish someone would fall off a roof and break a leg, or get fired and go bankrupt, or have trouble with the kids, we are like the disciples who wanted to call down fire to destroy the Samaritan village. Jesus rebuked James and John, saying, "You do not know what manner of spirit you are of. For the Son of Man did not come to destroy men's lives but to save them" (verses 55–56). The spirit James and John were operating in was altogether different from the Spirit of God. Jesus was telling them, "You are being influenced by the devil."

The Spirit of God is operating in you when you want your offenders to get right with God. You want them to repent and be blessed. If they are not saved, you want them to accept Jesus as Lord and be filled with the Spirit. You want their families and their marriages to prosper; you want things to go well in their lives. The Son of Man did not come to destroy men's lives but to save them. If that is not your passion, bitterness has created in you the wrong spirit, a vengeful spirit, which will spring up and begin to motivate your actions.

A Rebellious Spirit

One of the worst consequences of bitterness is that it creates rebellion inside you. The Bible illustrates this in several places, but let's look at Ephesians 6:1–4 (italics added):

> Children, obey your parents in the Lord, for this is right. *"Honor your father and mother,"* which is the first commandment with promise: *"that it may be well with you and you may live long on the earth."* And you, fathers, do not provoke your children to wrath, but bring them up in the training and admonition of the Lord.

Notice the admonition to parents: "Do not provoke your children to wrath." The reason for this is it sets the stage for rebellion. To "provoke your children to wrath" or to "exasperate them to resentment" (AMP) is to allow seeds of bitterness in their hearts. We can do that by saying one thing and living another—if we tell them to tell the truth and then they see us lie to the landlord . . . if we scold them for using bad language and yet curse and swear when things don't go our way . . . if we tell them not to smoke while puffing away. . . . It is easy for children to get disgusted at "unfair" expectations from a parent who demands behavior that he or she is unwilling to model for them. Disgust is "baby bitterness."

I think we can also "exasperate them to resentment" by just plain neglect. Children need a parent's guidelines, instruction, correction, loving attention, approval and affection. When we live our lives ignoring their needs while we selfishly take care of our own, we provoke or "set the stage" for resentment in their hearts. We allow them to think they have a "right" to be angry at us for not meeting their needs and to justify filling their trunks with resentment. But resentment is also "baby bitterness."

Disgust, resentment, holding grudges—these open the door to bitterness, which produces rebellion. It is the beginning of an attitude of rejection and hatred. Children will be angry and resentful toward you, and they will often reject whatever you stand for. If you are a Christian, they may rebel by rejecting your Christian values.

One way *not* to provoke children to wrath is to ask for forgiveness and teach them to forgive. It is not as though we as parents will never make mistakes. Equipping them by example and words to release those resentments instead of packing them away in their trunks will go far in keeping rebellion away.

75

The Bible says "rebellion is as the sin of witchcraft" (1 Samuel 15:23). It is a deadly, deadly action. As with anger, you cannot focus rebellion. There are three areas of authority: divine, governmental and parental. A person cannot choose to rebel only in certain areas; rebellion spills over everywhere. If he rebels against his parents, he will be a problem in school. If she rebels against God, she will have a hard time obeying an officer of the law. Rebellion is rebellion across the board.

Since rebellion is as the sin of witchcraft, it also lays your life wide open to demonic attack. Few things open your life to the devil the way witchcraft does! That is one reason Hebrews 12:15 says many become "defiled" when they let a root of bitterness spring up. A bitter spirit always produces rebellion and allows Satan to defile your life.

The word *defiled* means soiled, filthy or polluted. You cannot get something clean out of a dirty vessel. If you put clean water in a dirty cup, then no matter how sparkling pure the water was, it will become dirty. When you become defiled, it does not matter what else you have inside, you are still defiled, and everything that comes out of you is defiled. James 3:10–11 says, "Out of the same mouth proceed blessing and cursing. My brethren, these things ought not to be so. Does a spring send forth fresh water and bitter from the same opening?" Either you are a clean vessel producing good things or you are not.

The Bitterness Trap

Do not let bitterness take root in you and defile you. It will create more kinds of junk in your trunk than you can ever imagine. It can turn you into a whiner and force you to exhaust yourself emotionally. It can give you a taste for strife and gossip. It can create a vengeful or rebellious attitude in you and bring with it many other companion issues. Hanging on to bitterness in your trunk can cause such a hardening of attitudes that your mind becomes like cement—all mixed up and permanently set (at least until it is renewed by the Word).

Bitterness will trap you in ways you may not foresee, and its companions will be harder to break loose from than you bargained for. I often repeat to my church something I heard John Osteen say years ago: "Sin will take you farther than you want to go, keep you longer than you planned to stay and cost you more than you're prepared to pay." You can substitute the word *bitterness* for the word *sin* in that sentence, for they are the same and the result is the same.

Unloading Your Trunk

1. How many days in a week do you feel emotionally exhausted? Are you playing the *Look How They Hurt Me* movie in your mind before falling asleep? Try a new approach. Pray for your offenders as you lie down: "Lord, by faith I forgive them. Lord, bless them with all the blessings I ask for my own life. Grant them repentance and save them." Then try what Psalm 63:6 suggests: "I meditate on You in the night watches." Fall asleep meditating on a favorite Scripture passage and see how much more physical and emotional energy you have the next day.

2. Do you examine your motives before relating news of an offense? Do you feel reluctance and sorrow about bringing the offense to a third party's attention? Do they have authority to correct the situation? Then your news may be a necessary report. Or do you feel

a tingle of anticipation and urgency about spreading your news? Are you approaching a third party who cannot bring resolution and justifying yourself by "asking them to pray"? You may be justifying gossip. Think twice before participating in something the Lord considers an abomination.

3. Did you go through a rebellious stage against your parents? What did they do that provoked you to wrath and bitterness? Have you forgiven them? If not, do that now. Rebellion is as the sin of witchcraft, so you also need to close any doors you opened to satanic influence. If you are a Christian, use the spiritual authority you have in Jesus' name to tell the devil he is through in your life and to command him and his demonic influences to leave. If you are not sure how to do that, see the "Four Steps to Forgiveness" section in chapter 12. The fourth step gives an example of what to do. If you are not a Christian, first pray the prayer in the "Possessing the Ultimate Treasure" section of chapter 12 to settle your salvation. You will then have the necessary spiritual authority to close the door firmly on the devil!

7

A Tale of Two Trunks
King Saul

One man was exalted and powerful, the first king over God's chosen nation. He had great wealth and an army at his disposal. The other man was oppressed and powerless, a slave and prisoner in a pagan land. He was sold away by brothers who hated him and jailed because of his master's spiteful wife. Which man would best fulfill God's purposes in history? Which man would affect the lives of countless thousands for good and leave a rich spiritual inheritance to future generations?

The king had every advantage; he seemed to be headed toward a glorious future. The slave had less than nothing; he seemed to be headed toward a terrible end. Still, the answer is not as obvious as it seems. An important variable would greatly influence the outcome of their lives: Much would depend on which man carried junk in his trunk.

In our lives as well, much depends on whether or not we carry junk in our trunks. It can determine the outcome of our spiritual race. Will we finish or will we fail? Will we accomplish God's purposes for us? Will we pass on spiritual poverty or riches? Each decision we make to pick up or pass by an offense affects the amount of junk in our trunks. How important is that variable? We can learn the answer from the two men described above, King Saul and Joseph.

In this chapter, we will examine the contents of King Saul's trunk, so to speak, by looking at how he reacted to offense. Then in the next chapter, we will examine the contents of Joseph's trunk by looking at what he did with his numerous opportunities to become offended. Scripture shows us how the decisions of these two Old Testament characters affected whether or not they carried junk in their trunks. It also shows us how that variable, in turn, greatly influenced the outcome of their lives.

Make Room for Junk

Even before he became king, Saul had a lot going for him. Scripture describes him for us:

Kish the son of Abiel . . . had a choice and handsome son whose name was Saul. There was not a more handsome person than he among the children of Israel. From his shoulders upward he was taller than any of the people.

1 Samuel 9:1–2

Choice, handsome and tall—even in today's society that is enough to give Saul the advantage. But there is more:

Samuel took a flask of oil and poured it on his [Saul's] head, and kissed him and said: "Is it not because the LORD has anointed you commander over His inheritance? . . . You

80

shall come to the hill of God … you will meet a group of prophets coming down from the high place with a stringed instrument, a tambourine, a flute, and a harp before them; and they will be prophesying. Then the Spirit of the LORD will come upon you, and you will prophesy with them and be turned into another man."

1 Samuel 10:1, 5–6

Besides physical advantage, Saul was given spiritual advantage, too. The prophet Samuel anointed him, the Spirit of the Lord came upon him and he was "turned into another man"—God made him a new person on the inside. Talk about a trunkload of treasure!

Saul's future looked glorious indeed. And then came that little incident we mentioned in chapter 4, where the women greeted the returning army by singing about Saul slaying his thousands and David his ten thousands. Saul could not let it pass by—it just needled his pride—and he picked up offense toward David. He let the sun go down on that anger, and the very next day an evil spirit came. Saul opened the door to the devil by packing the junk of offense in his trunk. Like dirt and clean water, trash and treasure do not go well together. When you take the purest water on earth and add a little dirt to it, which substance changes the most in quality? Right. Things were bound to get messy in Saul's trunk.

What You Lose First

True friendships and important relationships are the first treasures you tarnish when you place bitterness in your trunk. When you get bitter, you lose the people most important to you. People find it hard to stay around someone who is full of poison. Even if the poison is not directed at them, they know it will affect them negatively.

Although Saul was poisoned with bitterness toward David, notice in 1 Samuel 20 how it affected his family: "Then Saul's anger was aroused against Jonathan, and he said to him, 'You son of a perverse, rebellious woman!'" (verse 30). Saul's jealousy of David ignited anger in his heart that burned those closest to him—his wife and son, the very son for whom he was trying to preserve the throne! Saul thought preserving the throne required killing David, so he chastised Jonathan:

> "Do I not know that you have chosen the son of Jesse to your own shame and to the shame of your mother's nakedness? For as long as the son of Jesse lives on the earth, you shall not be established, nor your kingdom. Now therefore, send and bring him to me, for he shall surely die."
>
> verses 30–31

Jonathan loved his father, but he loved David, too. He answered, "Why should he be killed? What has he done?" (verse 32). When you are bitter, the people who really love you will confront you about it. Proverbs 27:5–6 says, "Open rebuke is better than love carefully concealed. Faithful are the wounds of a friend." A person who loves you will try to correct you. Suppose you arrive at the office with a "crusty" in your nose. Your coworkers know you have an important meeting coming up, but they let you walk around with that somewhat offensive object visible all day. Do they love you? Nope. Someone who cares will say, "Hey, hit the restroom and take care of that thing in your nose before your meeting." It may embarrass you, but faithful are the wounds of a friend!

Instead of receiving Jonathan's correction, Saul rejected it and even tried to kill his own son and heir:

> Saul cast a spear at him to kill him, by which Jonathan knew that it was determined by his father to kill David. So Jonathan arose from the table in fierce anger . . . for he was grieved for David, because his father had treated him shamefully.
>
> 1 Samuel 20:33–34

Jonathan knew his father's actions were shameful. Sometimes if a bitter person will not receive correction, you have to separate yourself from him or her. Jonathan did just that, and Saul lost his relationship with his son. "Reproofs of instruction are the way of life," Proverbs 6:23 says, but if we are not willing to be corrected, we can lose the ones closest to us who are trying to help us.

Saul's attitude lost him several precious relationships. David, who only honored and served Saul, could not come anywhere near him. Jonathan and his mother were affected. The prophet Samuel had already distanced himself because of Saul's disobedience and behaviors: "And Samuel went no more to see Saul until the day of his death. Nevertheless Samuel mourned for Saul" (1 Samuel 15:35).

Quality people separate themselves from the poison of bitterness. They don't want anything to do with that kind of junk—or the people who spread it.

Losing Focus on God's Purpose

Making room for junk tarnished more than Saul's relationships. It also muddied his focus on God's purpose for him as king. Remember, focus is tremendously powerful:

The focused light of a laser beam can cut through steel. If you know God's purpose for your life and focus your energies into fulfilling it, you will run your spiritual race with excellence. But you can focus in only one direction. God didn't put eyes in the back of your head. If you decide to focus on a bitter root of unforgiveness, you will lose your focus on God and His purpose. More people probably fail because of misdirected focus than because of any other reason.

You cannot focus both on God's plan and on bitterness. You cannot have both in your trunk. Saul couldn't either, and he chose the junk. When Saul became king, he had a purpose: The king was to protect the land, to bring social improvements to the land and to judge the people of the land. But on the day Saul picked up offense, his focus changed from God's purpose to getting revenge. Scripture says that "Saul became David's enemy continually" (1 Samuel 18:29), and that Saul sought David every day to destroy him (see 1 Samuel 23:14).

Saul kept a closer eye on David than on the kingdom! Instead of protecting the land, he was going around and around a mountain trying to catch and kill David. He was on one side of the mountain and David was on the other, and it was like a merry-go-round until Saul's men reported that the Philistines had invaded the land. Saul stopped chasing David in order to go fight the Philistines, but if he had been doing what he was *supposed* to be doing in the first place, it is possible they never would have invaded the land.

Saul was also supposed to use his position as king to bring social improvements to the land. Later on under David's and then Solomon's administration, Israel went through tremendous improvements. But under King Saul's administration, how many improvements were made? Scripture records none. Zero. Why? Saul lost his focus. Instead of fulfilling his destiny and purpose, he was obsessed with finding and punishing David, a man who had done him no wrong.

Losing the Fear of God

Then there was the matter of judging the people. In his reign later, King Solomon immediately began to hand down incredibly wise judgments. Remember the story of the two women brought before him who both claimed parental rights to the same child? He directed that the boy be cut in two and half be given to each woman because he knew the real mother would forsake her claim so her son could live. When she did so, Solomon rewarded her with the child (see 1 Kings 3:16–28). Solomon's focus was on his kingly purpose. King Saul, however, was too consumed with bitterness to take the time to judge the people.

In the forty years Saul was king, the Bible records very few times he made a judgment, and those judgments were a sad indictment against him. One was a terrible travesty of justice against a priest's household, and it showed that Saul had lost more than his focus on God's purpose. In his bitterness, he had even lost his fear of God. Once again David was on the run from Saul's murderous wrath. David went to the priest Ahimelech at Nob and asked for food, and the priest inquired of the Lord for him. He also gave David bread and the sword of Goliath, whom David had slain. The priest knew that David had always done only good to Saul, and David said he was about the king's business. The priest had every reason to help him.

Looking for David, Saul complained to his servants, "All of you have conspired against me, . . . and there is not one of you who is sorry for me or reveals to me that my son [Jonathan] has stirred up my servant against me, to lie in wait, as it is this day" (1 Samuel 22:8). Now, Saul's servants were not all conspiring against him, but when you let bitterness grow inside, you begin to feel isolated and alone. You begin to act like a victim; nothing is your fault and everyone else is to blame. When you make room for a victim mentality in your trunk, treasures like friendship get tossed out, as we have already seen. People just do not like to attend a pity party unless the party is for them! Saul was having a pity party here, telling his men, "None of you feels sorry for me, you are all against me—nobody likes me, everybody hates me, I'm going to go eat worms. . . ."

Despite his woe-is-me attitude, Saul was not being victimized, nor was David lying in wait to kill him. David, in fact, had ample opportunity to kill Saul during their little game around the mountain. At one point he sneaked up and cut off the corner of Saul's robe just to prove that he meant Saul no harm. And David's conscience greatly troubled him about doing even that much! He told his men, "The LORD forbid that I should do this thing to my master, the LORD's anointed, to stretch out my hand against him, seeing he is the anointed of the LORD" (1 Samuel 24:6). In all his struggles as the undeserved object of Saul's hatred, David never once allowed himself to pick up offense against King Saul, nor did he lose his fear of God.

Not so with Saul. His bitterness kept him from thinking straight. He determined that *somebody's* head was going to roll, and since David was out of reach, he started accusing his own men of conspiracy (again, so much for focused anger). These poor servants had an angry, irrational king on their hands, and they knew somebody better *do* something fast, or heads would be rolling everywhere! One man who happened to witness David's exchange with Ahimelech the priest stepped up to volunteer information: "I saw the son of Jesse going to Nob, to Ahimelech the son of Ahitub. And he inquired of the LORD for him, gave him provisions, and gave him the sword of Goliath the Philistine" (1 Samuel 22:9–10). That turned Saul's focus from his servants, no doubt to their vast relief—but it was not so good for his new target, the priests.

Hearing this report, King Saul summoned Ahimelech the priest and all his father's house, the priests in Nob. When they appeared, Saul voiced his victim refrain again:

"Why have you conspired against me, you and the son of Jesse, in that you have given him bread and a sword, and have inquired of God for him, that he should rise against me, to lie in wait, as it is this day?"

1 Samuel 22:13

This audience with King Saul was not like anything the priests had anticipated. Taken aback, Ahimelech answered,

"And who among all your servants is as faithful as David, who is the king's son-in-law, who goes at your bidding, and is honorable in your house? Did I then begin to inquire of God for him? Far be it from me! Let not the king impute anything to his servant, or to any in the house of my father. For your servant knew nothing of all this, little or much."

1 Samuel 22:14–15

The priests have done no wrong, but Saul is bitter. Bitterness prevents you from seeing things clearly. You are wearing those blinders we talked about in chapter 2, and you become deceived. You filter everything through your insecurity and bitterness, and you are unable to judge a situation properly. Saul's blind judgment is horrible: "You shall surely die, Ahimelech, you and all your father's house!" (verse 16).

Saul ordered his guards to kill all the priests, and despite his dangerous state of mind, they actually refused! "The servants of the king would not lift their hands to strike the priests of the LORD" (verse 17). Like David, they had not lost their fear of God. But the informant, Doeg, an Edomite, had no such qualms. He

> killed on that day eighty-five men who wore a linen ephod. Also Nob, the city of the priests, he struck with the edge of the sword, both men and women, children and nursing infants, oxen and donkeys and sheep—with the edge of the sword.
>
> verses 18–19

Eighty-five priests of the Lord, their wives, their children, even their livestock were dead because Saul was bitter toward David.

Bitterness is deadly. It always destroys. It always defiles. Making room for bitterness in his trunk forced Saul to take out some of his most valuable treasures: good judgment; true friendships and important relationships; focus on God's purpose; even his fear of God. Eventually he lost his kingdom and his life. Saul lost far more than he gained. We would be wise not to make the same exchange.

Unloading Your Trunk

1. Every decision we make to pass by or pick up offense affects the amount of junk we carry in our trunks. The last time you had opportunity to become offended, were you like Saul? Did you tarnish valuable treasures

by adding trash? If so, it is not too late to do some cleaning. Reread the "Anyone and Anything" section at the end of chapter 4, then forgive by faith. Make a firm decision that the next time offense is offered, you will not pick it up. You will pass it by.

2. Have you ever walked away from a friend who could not get past bitterness at someone else? How did the poison in your friend affect you? Did you try to correct your friend? What about your behavior toward those closest to you? If a friend or loved one has tried to correct you recently, how did you receive it? If you value your relationship, accept loving reproof. Keep in mind that "faithful are the wounds of a friend."

3. I recently asked a pastor from a somewhat closed-minded group what he thought of Billy Graham. "He's going to hell," the man replied. I made sure we were both thinking of the same evangelist. "Yes," he insisted, "I tell you, he's going to hell!" David knew better than to touch God's anointed, but Saul had lost his fear of God. What about you and me? When we see something in the Body of Christ that we don't understand, are we being careful before we condemn it? God doesn't need our permission to do something new or different. He might involve us, or He might not. If He does not, we need to avoid the jealousy that plagued Saul over David's successes. We need to avoid speaking or acting against someone else whom God is blessing.

8

A Tale of Two Trunks
Joseph

Joseph, like Saul, was another choice and handsome son in the Bible who had a lot going for him at the start. In his case, though, it didn't last.

At a young age Joseph found himself stripped of home, family and his famous multicolored coat. Standing naked on an auction block in Egypt, he was sold into slavery. The iron chains around his neck, hands and feet were only the beginning of his troubles. He lost everything overnight, or nearly everything. He did hang on to one thing in the midst of his disaster—the treasures in his trunk. Let's take a look inside at what Joseph carried—and what he refused to carry. As with Saul, the contents of Joseph's trunk would make all the difference in his final outcome.

Although Joseph was the eleventh of twelve sons in the family of Jacob, his father "loved Joseph more than all his children, because he was the son of his old age" (Genesis

37:3). Jacob also gave Joseph a beautiful coat, the famous coat of many colors. By the time Joseph was seventeen, he was clearly the favorite son. Like Saul, Joseph seemed to be headed for a glorious future.

If you want trouble in your household, show one of your children favoritism! Genesis 37:4 relates that "when his brothers saw that their father loved him more than all his brothers, they hated him and could not speak peaceably to him." They could not bear to talk to the boy—but that did not stop Joseph from talking to them. He wasn't overly tactful, either. He described a couple of dreams in which he was ruler of his entire family. In one his father, mother and brothers were the sun, the moon and the eleven stars, and they were all bowing down to *him*. This did not help his standing: "They hated him even more for his dreams and for his words." Even his father rebuked him: "What is this dream that you have dreamed? Shall your mother and I and your brothers indeed come to bow down to the earth before you?" (Genesis 37:8, 10).

Sometimes when God tells you something, it is better not to tell anyone else—just be wise and keep your mouth shut. Joseph had not learned this lesson yet, and his brothers were not happy about his dreams of grandeur. They decided he needed a rude awakening.

No Room for Junk

One day Jacob sent Joseph to check on his brothers, who were feeding the flock in Shechem. Once before, Joseph had delivered a bad report to Jacob. This time, the brothers were not about to let that happen again. When they saw Joseph in the distance, they said to one another,

"Look, this dreamer is coming! Come therefore, let us now kill him and cast him into some pit; and we shall say, 'Some wild beast has devoured him.' We shall see what will become of his dreams!"

Genesis 37:19–20

They stripped off the boy's fancy coat and would have murdered him, except that brother Reuben thought better of it and intervened. When a caravan of Ishmaelites passed by, the rest of them, in Reuben's absence, rid themselves of Joseph. They sold the dreamer off for twenty shekels of silver, or about $12.80 according to *Dake's Annotated Reference Bible.*

I could write a book about the junk Joseph's brothers carried in *their* trunks. They had spent years stuffing in offense toward Joseph and their father, Jacob. They were overloaded with hatred and were cultivating a whole crop of bitter spiritual fruit. After they stripped Joseph, tossed him in a pit and sold him into slavery, they dipped his fancy coat in goat's blood, presented it to their father and *lied* to him:

"We have found this. Do you know whether it is your son's tunic or not?" And he recognized it and said, "It is my son's tunic. A wild beast has devoured him. Without doubt Joseph is torn to pieces." Then Jacob tore his clothes, put sackcloth on his waist, and mourned for his son many days . . . and he said, "For I shall go down into the grave to my son in mourning."

Genesis 37:32–35

Those guys watched grief nearly kill Jacob, and they did *nothing*! In his great distress they did not tell the truth. They had thrown integrity and compassion out of their trunks to make room inside for bitterness.

93

Joseph could easily have done the same. If your brothers hated you, mocked you, beat you and sold you as a slave, you might have a thing or two to deal with, right? Joseph probably had more opportunities than any of us to pick up offense. With brothers like those, he did not need enemies! He had all the reasons he needed to become bitter and vengeful. You might imagine that he grew into a miserable, hateful young man, but what happened in Egypt? Just the opposite—Joseph became fruitful and on his way up again! (At least temporarily.) He was purchased by Potiphar, an officer of Pharaoh, and Scripture tells what became of Joseph the slave:

> He was a successful man. . . . And his master saw that the LORD was with him and that the LORD made all he did to prosper in his hand. So Joseph found favor in his sight, and served him. Then he made him overseer of his house, and all that he had he put under his authority. So it was, from the time that he had made him overseer of his house and all that he had, that the LORD blessed the Egyptian's house for Joseph's sake; and the blessing of the LORD was on all that he had in the house and in the field.
>
> Genesis 39:2–5

Joseph obviously refused to allow a root of bitterness to spoil his life. A bitter, hateful spirit doesn't prosper, but the blessing of the Lord was all over Joseph in Egypt! He kept his integrity, served his new master well and was successful in everything. He was too busy being fruitful to pack junk into his trunk. But another opportunity to pick up offense awaited him. . . .

Bypassing Junk and Becoming Fruitful

Like Saul, Joseph was "handsome in form and appearance" (Genesis 39:6). While handsome Joseph was busy keeping an eye on Potiphar's household, Potiphar's wife was busy keeping an eye on him. She cast longing eyes on him and soon she began asking him day after day to lie with her. No doubt she was beautiful, and many a man in Joseph's low position would grab whatever pleasure and advantage he could get. Bitter people often figure life owes them something after all they have been through. Yet notice Joseph's response to her:

> "My master . . . has committed all that he has to my hand. There is no one greater in this house than I, nor has he kept back anything from me but you, because you are his wife. How then can I do this great wickedness, and sin against God?"
>
> Genesis 39:8–9

Joseph displayed the treasure of integrity in his trunk. Rather than resenting his master, Joseph determined not to disappoint him. Rather than blaming God for his circumstances, Joseph determined not to sin against Him.

For his integrity, Joseph earned some jail time. One day Potiphar's wife grabbed him by his garment and *begged* him to lie with her. The Bible says none of the household's men were inside. Joseph could easily have given in. Instead, he fled from her and from sin, leaving his garment in her hand. Now, the woman was powerful as well as beautiful, and she was humiliated by his continual refusals. When her husband arrived home, she showed him Joseph's garment and lied (the same trick Joseph's brothers pulled on Jacob!). She claimed Joseph tried to take advantage of her but fled without his garment when she screamed. Though Potiphar thought highly of Joseph, he fell for his wife's story. (Proverbs 6:34–35 says that jealousy is a husband's fury and nothing will appease it.) Joseph landed in the king's prison for a crime he did not commit, and he was forgotten for years—maybe it would be forever. . . .

Suppose you were a young man torn from home and family, stripped naked, bound with chains and sold at a slave auction. You work hard to please your new master, overseeing and prospering his entire household. You even refuse to sleep with his beautiful wife, though she throws herself at you over and over. In return for your faithful and outstanding service, your master buys into her false accusations. He finds you guilty of the very thing you ran away from, tosses you into prison and throws away the key. You might have a thing or two to deal with after all that, right?

That is exactly where Joseph found himself. Every effort to overcome extreme adversity seemed to land him in continually worse circumstances. Now his life appeared to be over as he waited to die in a miserable hole of a dungeon. You might think that Joseph would carry a chip on his shoulder the size of all Egypt. No more Mr. Nice Guy! From now on, he would probably load his trunk with all kinds of bitter junk and finally start looking out for number one.

Not Joseph. He forgave his brothers, and he forgave Potiphar and his wife. Forgiveness is the only explanation for his attitude in prison. Rather than be miserable and mean, Joseph used his time and talents to improve the prison!

> The keeper of the prison committed to Joseph's hand all the prisoners who were in the prison; whatever they did there, it was his doing. The keeper of the prison did not

look into anything that was under Joseph's authority, because the LORD was with him; and whatever he did, the LORD made it prosper.

Genesis 39:22–23

Again, Joseph was too busy being fruitful to load his trunk with junk; he was free to see the needs of those around him. With God's help and blessing, Joseph was able, in the middle of awful circumstances, to minister successfully to the other prisoners—including the king's butler and baker who had offended their lord and been imprisoned. One day as Joseph served them, he noticed they were downcast. Bitter people are self-centered. Not Joseph. He took note of other prisoners' troubles instead of dwelling on his own. Joseph "asked Pharaoh's officers who were with him in the custody of his lord's house, saying, 'Why do you look so sad today?'" (Genesis 40:7).

Joseph had not forgotten the wrongs done to him—he suffered their consequences every day. But he had forgiven his offenders, which kept his trunk junk free and enabled him to serve others. The butler and baker told Joseph their trouble: They could not interpret their dreams. Joseph replied that dreams belong to God and offered to interpret the dreams for them. The butler's dream indicated that he would be restored to his former position, and Joseph asked him a favor:

> "Remember me when it is well with you, and please show kindness to me; make mention of me to Pharaoh, and get me out of this house. For indeed I was stolen away from the land of the Hebrews; and also I have done nothing here that they should put me into the dungeon."

Genesis 40:14–15

The butler regained his freedom but forgot about Joseph, and two whole years went by! Another huge opportunity for Joseph to take offense, but as always, he was too busy being fruitful.

Finally Pharaoh himself had a dream no one could interpret, and suddenly a light went on in the mind of the butler. He told Pharaoh about the young Hebrew prisoner who interpreted dreams accurately, and in fewer than 24 hours, Joseph went from prisoner to prime minister of the most powerful nation on earth.

God can change lives, just like that. He can get you, too, anywhere on planet Earth in 24 hours. Your life could be so different 24 hours from now that it would stagger your mind—assuming you are not so busy with the junk in your trunk that you miss what God has for you! Joseph was not swayed by bitterness, and God was able to give him immeasurable fruitfulness.

The Treasure of a Godly Attitude

One particular treasure in Joseph's trunk—his attitude—went a long way toward enabling God to fulfill His purposes for him—and through him. Sometimes attitude is everything. Notice Joseph's attitude before Pharaoh:

> Then Pharaoh sent and called Joseph, and they brought him quickly out of the dungeon; and he shaved, changed his clothing, and came to Pharaoh. And Pharaoh said to Joseph, "I have had a dream, and there is no one who can interpret it. But I have heard it said of you that you can understand a dream, to interpret it." So Joseph answered Pharaoh, saying, "It is not in me; God will give Pharaoh an answer of peace."
>
> Genesis 41:14–16

Joseph could have reacted with anger—"Why should I, a slave in *your* country, interpret a dream for *you*? I've been thrown into *your* prison for something I didn't do. Find someone else to help!" He probably would not have been appointed prime minister by that route, though. He might even have found himself minus his head. Bitterness is deadly.

Joseph also could have reacted by looking out for number one—"I *could* interpret for you, Pharaoh, but first, what's in it for *me*? You help me, and I'll help you. I want my freedom!" That kind of wheedling probably would not have gotten him the prime minister position either. Self-centeredness is unattractive.

Instead, Joseph pulled the treasure of a godly attitude out of his trunk. Humbling himself and giving glory to God, he told Pharaoh, "It is not in me. God will give Pharaoh an answer" (Genesis 41:16). More than that, Joseph said it would be "an answer of peace." He wanted Pharaoh to find the answer he was looking for *and* find peace! Not only did Joseph interpret Pharaoh's dream, which signaled seven years of famine in the future, but he suggested a plan to protect Egypt and safeguard the lives of its people. He was more concerned with Pharaoh's good than with his own.

Pharaoh took notice of Joseph's attitude, exclaiming to his servants, "Can we find such a one as this, a man in whom is the Spirit of God?" (Genesis 41:38). He put Joseph in charge of carrying out the proposed plan, saying, "You shall be over my house, and all my people shall be ruled according to your word; only in regard to the throne will I be greater than you" (Genesis 41:40).

No Passion for Revenge

Pharaoh's favor toward Joseph had to make a few people sit up and take notice—Potiphar, his wife and the king's chief butler, for instance. Joseph could have used his new position to take revenge on them. The first order many of us would have given in his place is "Bring that Mrs. Potiphar in here! Make sure her husband comes, too. Then find the chief butler. . . ." But Joseph didn't do that.

As the second-highest official in Egypt, Joseph could probably have taken revenge on his family, too. But he did not do so even when his brothers finally came to Egypt. (He did not trust them, having learned a lesson or two along the way. He made them demonstrate some fruit of their repentance. But that is another story.) It is clear that Joseph said not a word about their evil actions. He never whined to Pharaoh, "These are the rotten brothers who sold me into slavery—off with their heads!" When the Egyptian officials heard Joseph's family was coming, in fact, they welcomed them excitedly! Joseph had covered his brothers' sins.

Joseph simply refused to nurse a passion for revenge. He stayed too busy being fruitful to get agitated about getting even. The king gave him a wife, and he named their first son Manasseh, roughly meaning "For God has made me forget all my toil and all my father's house" (Genesis 41:51). If you want the blessing of God on your life, do what Joseph did—he forgave, and he forgot all his pain caused by the people who wronged him. We talked earlier about how Paul said to forget those things that are behind. You can mull over other people's offenses again and again in your mind and relive the hurt every day. Or you can forgive them, release the past and live your best life wherever you are, as Joseph did.

Joseph named his second son Ephraim, roughly meaning "For God has caused me to be fruitful in the land of my affliction" (Genesis 41:52). If you want to be fruitful, do what Joseph did—forgive, forget and go on. You cannot carry bitterness and have a fruitful life.

All the Difference in the World

Every person I know has had something done to him or her that hurt cruelly and was wrong. I do not know anyone who is an exception. We have all been wronged, but whether or not we pick up an offense can make all the difference in our outcomes. Saul was king of God's chosen nation and everything was going his way. Then he filled his trunk with bitterness. It cost him a kingdom and eventually his life. Joseph was a forgotten prisoner in a pagan land and nothing was going his way. He refused to fill his trunk with bitterness. Instead he displayed the treasures of forgiveness, integrity and a godly attitude. Joseph gained a kingdom and regained his life. In fact, he preserved the lives of untold thousands: "All countries came to Joseph in Egypt to buy grain, because the famine was severe in all lands" (Genesis 41:57). He literally influenced the outcome of the whole world! He could not have done it with junk in his trunk.

Unloading Your Trunk

1. What might have happened if King Saul and Joseph had traded trunks? Suppose King Saul had been glad of David's successes and had followed God's lead for the kingdom. Would Old Testament history record

a different outcome for his life? Suppose Joseph had been consumed with hatred toward his brothers and toward Potiphar's household. If Joseph had been a rebellious slave and an unruly prisoner, how might his story have unfolded differently? How might your story unfold differently if you decide to change the contents of your trunk?

2. Are you facing any situations where things looked good at the start, but now they are going straight downhill? Step back and think about how your reaction to the circumstances and the people behind them might affect you in the long run. Think about where King Saul and Joseph ended up because of their reactions to offense. Decide which man's example you will follow based on what you would like your final outcome to be.

3. Joseph had much bigger opportunities to pick up offense than most of us will ever face. Why do you think he did so well at bypassing offenses? Was it because even in the "land of his affliction" he was too busy being fruitful? Even in prison he was too busy focusing on blessing others to worry about nursing a grudge! When you are tempted to pick up offense, first forgive and pray for your offender, then focus on how you can bless someone else. You may be surprised at how fruitful you can be, even in the "land of your affliction."

4. Joseph displayed treasures like integrity and a godly attitude, which helped him through his rough times. What treasures do you display in times of difficulty? Can you think of any treasures you would like to add to your trunk to aid you in the future? What does Scripture say about developing them?

9

Bitter to the Bone

Where He leads me, I will follow.
All they feed me, I will swallow.

That parody of an old hymn is passed around among missionaries as a reminder to go where they are led and not be picky about what they are fed. So even though my friend and I literally could not see the ceiling above us because of its blanket of flies, we ate—and we paid a price with our health. One of us paid a higher price than the other, though, and I believe the cost was directly related to what we had in our trunks.

Jeanie and I were missionaries in Mexico at the time, and a pastor friend of ours was helping me tremendously by teaching me a great deal about the ministry. He even taught me how to tie a Windsor knot so I could wear a tie! Besides the little church Jeanie and I were starting, his church was the very first one I preached in. As often as I could, I helped him by preaching for him. It was on one such occasion that he and I decided to travel to a little village, *un ranchito*, where the villagers had just broken ground on my friend's 33rd church. He was so excited about it that he said, "I just have to take you out there and show you the site!" Off we went to visit the new church.

When we arrived, some church members spotted us walking around the construction site and rushed over to greet us. "We're *so* glad you're here! Please, come have something to eat with us," they urged. We followed them home, and there the missionary song started playing in my head. I have stayed in some truly humble abodes, places with thatched roofs, no electricity and nothing more than a dirt floor. This house, though, was the dirtiest place I have ever, and I mean *ever*, set foot in. When the people brought us the food, we had to wave our hands to shoe away the flies so we could tell what kind of bread it was, brown or black. It was so, so dirty. But "all they feed me, I will swallow." My friend and I ate what they offered.

A few months later, I gave my pastor friend a call, but could not reach him. We were supposed to travel together again, this time to Lakewood Church where John Osteen had a missions convention scheduled, but I discovered my friend was very sick and had been hospitalized. His condition went from bad to worse, and in a matter of days he passed away.

At this same time, I experienced an attack on my health. I had no idea what I was fighting. I went from bad to worse, too. My skin and the whites of my eyes turned a horrible yellowish green, and my liver was grossly inflamed. My urine was bright red, and my stools were white. When I saw the doctor his report was serious: "You have hepatitis and could die."

Jeanie and I turned fervently to God's Word, praying and thanking Him for my healing. The next morning, I still had no strength. I could barely walk or keep any food down, but I forced myself to get up and get going. After lunch I came home and dropped into bed. By that evening, though, I was healed and I was playing basketball.

God had *completely* healed me. Recently I underwent a thorough physical for an insurance policy. My blood test results came back completely negative—no hepatitis!

I know God healed me, but my pastor friend died. We had both traveled to the place where we could not see the ceiling for the flies, we had both eaten the same fly-infested food and we had both suffered a severe attack on our bodies at the same time afterward. We also both served the same healing God, but still my friend died. He could have been completely healed as well. What happened? I could not understand it. His death deeply troubled me, so I asked the Lord, *Why?*

The Lord did not answer me directly, but He did bring something to my remembrance. My friend's church had gone through a split. Some of his congregation stirred up division, then they left and built another church only a quarter mile away. Every time I saw my friend, he talked about it. "You know what they did?" he would ask. The next time, he would say, "You know what they're doing now? They're calling and visiting all my church members. They're trying to steal our people!" Another time it might be, "They hurt me so much! They took so-and-so from me!"

As wonderful as my friend was, he never missed a chance to talk about the people who had done such an awful thing to him and his church. And it *was* an awful thing—Proverbs 16:28 says, "A perverse man sows strife, and a whisperer separates the best of friends." These people separated a

105

whole church body. But my friend never forgave them. When I asked the Lord why he died, all the Lord did was bring this to my remembrance.

As we discussed in chapter 4, when you don't forgive, the Bible says you give place to the devil. Satan has a foothold into your life. He may attack your family. He may attack your finances or your health. Whenever you allow any bitterness in your trunk, he *will* attack somewhere. Your immune systems—both spiritual and physical—will be weakened. I believe bitterness kept my friend from receiving God's healing grace.

The Trunk-Body Connection

No doubt about it, the state of your spiritual immune system affects your physical health. What you pack in your trunk affects your spiritual immune system. That makes for a definite trunk-body connection. Consider Proverbs 3:7–8: "Do not be wise in your own eyes; fear the LORD and depart from evil. It will be health to your flesh, and strength to your bones." You will be much healthier physically if you are not determined to go your own way, as we saw with Cain's self-interests. You will be much stronger in body if you have not abandoned your reverent fear of the Lord, as we saw with Saul's bitter judgment. Life or death could even be determined by your decision to forgive or hang on to unforgiveness, as I believe happened with my friend.

For the sake of your physical health, examine your trunk regularly and remove any junk! Proverbs 14:30 warns that bitterness is especially toxic to your health: "A calm and undisturbed mind and heart are the life and health of the body, but envy, jealousy, and wrath are like rottenness of the bones" (AMP). Peace of mind and heart bring life and health.

If, however, your mind is in constant turmoil because your heart is full of anger, you are headed for rottenness of the bones. *The Message* states it more graphically: "Runaway emotions corrode the bones." That is one picture I do not want my doctor showing me on my X-ray! I would rather keep the corrosive bitterness out of my trunk—and out of my bones.

I once read a true account of a woman who allowed bitterness deep in her bones. I hope that the gruesome act she needed to forgive is more than any of us will ever have to face. Her teenage daughter was abducted and murdered. One of the girl's teachers was responsible. This mother was absolutely devastated. She succumbed to despair, drank herself to sleep each night and neglected her other children. Hatred for the murderer consumed her, affecting her family life and her mental health. Soon it affected her physical health, too. She suffered constantly from headaches and back pains so severe that she could barely stand them.

After years of misery, the mother was attending a relative's funeral when a line from the Lord's Prayer pierced through her walls of hatred: "Forgive us our trespasses, as we forgive those who trespass against us" (see Matthew 6). She began an intensive study on forgiveness, reading everything she could about it. She became convinced that forgiveness was the answer to the mess she had made of her family and her health. First she began to tell herself over and over, "I'm willing to forgive my daughter's killer. I'm willing to forgive. . . ." Then she wrote the perpetrator a letter saying she would like to visit him. By now eleven years had gone by since the murder.

The mother visited the man in prison and poured out her heart, telling him how his crime had affected her. She related all she had lost and all she had been through. She wept brokenheartedly as she forgave him. He wept, too.

From that day forward, the junk in her trunk was gone, and so was the bitterness in her bones. Things began to turn around in her health and in her family. When some friends and acquaintances learned she had visited and forgiven the girl's killer, they were appalled, but she had no regrets. In fact, she stated that forgiveness was the greatest gift she had ever given herself or her family.

Opening a Door for God's Blessings Again

While bitterness opens the door for the enemy to attack our lives, forgiveness does just the opposite. Forgiveness is still its own reward—it is the best thing we can do for ourselves—but it also ushers in the blessings of God. When we forgive, we shut the door to the devil and we open a door for the blessings of God to flow into our lives again. This is especially true in regard to our physical health.

I have watched this happen time after time in people's lives. One of the most dramatic examples I have ever seen took place while Jeanie and I were still missionaries in Mexico. We had started a church in Guadalajara during our first two years, then we left it in the capable hands of a national pastor and moved to an Otomi Indian village across the country in Hidalgo. Meanwhile in Guadalajara, a prominent man in the congregation took great offense at the national pastor. One Sunday this man stormed down front to rant and rave at the pastor, then he stomped out, jumped in his car and squealed his tires down the road.

Eight months came and went. The man had not darkened the door of a church since the day of his tirade, but everywhere he went, he bad-mouthed the pastor: "That pastor, he's a false prophet. He's a wolf in sheep's clothes. He's a no-good liar. . . ."

By this time we had moved back to Guadalajara, and although I was not involved in that church anymore, I heard about what happened. It saddened me to see the effects one person's bitterness could have, but I decided to keep out of the situation. *I'm the former pastor now, and getting involved is just asking to get bitten*, I thought as I remembered Proverbs 26:17: "He who passes by and meddles in a quarrel not his own is like one who takes a dog by the ears."

One Sunday afternoon, however, Jeanie suggested that we visit this angry man and his wife. "Maybe later," I said, brushing it off. One of the things I hate most in life is confrontation, and I knew very well that I could not visit this couple without confronting the ugly situation between the man and his pastor.

Later Jeanie came to me again. "I think God wants us to go," she said.

After she told me how strongly she felt impressed that God wanted us to visit them, I could not shake the thought. I still procrastinated long enough so that by the time I said, "Let's go," Jeanie had put our son Joshua to bed for the night, so off I went alone.

At eight o'clock I knocked on the man's door. His wife was glad to see me and invited me inside. "My husband is upstairs in bed. Go on up," she said.

"In bed? At eight o'clock?" I questioned. No Latin person I knew went to bed so early—midnight, maybe, but not eight o'clock, which was just about time for some *tacos de lengua*, some cow-tongue tacos! Something was not right.

"So you don't know?" she asked.

"Know what?"

"He's going into the hospital tomorrow to have very serious surgery. He has a life-threatening tumor."

"I had no clue," I said.

I went upstairs. I should have known he would not be alone. At least twenty people were in the bedroom. In the Deep South of the U.S., when someone dies often the relatives hold a wake. They lay out the body at the house, and people come over and keep vigil. In the Latin culture, they do the same thing, but they do not wait until the person dies. They show love for a seriously ill person by staying with him or her in the sickroom.

Business acquaintances, relatives, people from the church—they all formed a horseshoe around the man's bed. I had come over hoping to confront the man about the ugly situation with his pastor. *I meant to talk with him privately and help bring resolution,* I told myself, *but I can't do it here. No way am I bringing it up in front of all these people! I'm going to say hello to him, talk with some people, and then I'm leaving.*

Another Latin custom is to shake everyone's hand when you arrive in a small room, and shake everyone's hand again when you leave. If you ignore the custom, you are considered rude, so I started shaking hands before leaving. About the third person I reached was this man's nephew, who attended our former church. "Aren't you at least going to pray for him?" he asked me loudly, putting me on the spot.

My initial reaction was to think, *No, I won't pray for him! What good will it do? He's full of resentment, bitterness and unforgiveness; he opened the door and gave place to the devil. I could lay hands on his head until I wear off every hair and it won't help. I might as well pray "Twinkle, twinkle little star, how I wonder what you are," because it's no use praying for this guy.*

But they all watched and waited, so I walked over to his bed. My mind shouted *Hypocrite!* while I prayed the nicest pastoral prayer I have ever prayed. It was *really* nice, but I knew nothing happened, he knew nothing happened and I think everybody in the room knew nothing happened.

110

The nephew certainly knew it. He ran downstairs when I concluded the prayer and was back before I could finish shaking hands. Pushing a huge container of cooking oil into my chest, he said, "Anoint him with oil like in James 5 in the Bible." Remember that Scripture?

> Is anyone among you sick? Let him call for the elders of the church, and let them pray over him, anointing him with oil in the name of the Lord. And the prayer of faith will save the sick, and the Lord will raise him up. And if he has committed sins, he will be forgiven.
>
> verses 14–15

I was left holding the oil and thinking, *This could be Crisco or Pennzoil or 3-in-1, and it wouldn't make any difference. It's not the oil that does the healing! It's faith, which can't work when his heart is not right.*

Oil is an important symbol. Scripture tells us, for instance, that when a priest in Israel turned thirty years old, he was anointed with oil. The oil was to be an outward symbol of what was happening in his heart as he dedicated himself to God. In effect, he was saying, "God, anything I'm doing that You don't want me to do, I'll quit. Anything You want of me that I'm not doing, I'll start." That is repentance—getting right with God in your heart. I certainly did not think anything like that was going on inside this sick man!

I leaned right over his bed and asked him discreetly, indirectly, "Could it be that, perhaps someplace, somewhere in your heart, you have something against somebody?"

The man looked right at me with fire in his eyes and said, "You know I do."

111

"Yes, I've heard a few things," I replied, "and it comes down to this: Do you want to be healed or do you want to have surgery?"

"What do you mean?"

"You will not be healed unless you forgive. Unforgiveness opens the door for Satan to come into your life. You have to forgive and allow God into your life again. If you'll do it, you can be healed."

It did not take him thirty seconds to decide, "I want to be healed!"

"You need to *forgive*," I insisted.

"I will. I will."

"All right. Close your eyes and forgive that person from your heart. Then ask God to forgive you for the bitterness you carried."

"Okay." He closed his eyes and prayed for less than a minute. "I did it. I forgave him," he announced. "As soon as I can, I'll go ask his forgiveness. I've been wrong."

That's a good sign, I told myself. I got the oil ready. In Bible college you learn to put a drop on your finger and place it on the person's forehead, but I confess my method that night was a bit extreme. As I took the top off this large container of oil, I had a few choice thoughts for him! *You turkey! For eight months you've been spewing out this bitterness and hatred. You opened the door for the devil, and here we both are.* So I poured out a huge dose of oil, *bloop, bloop*, into my palm, and I smeared it on him! I prayed in love, in faith, in Jesus' name. I shook more hands to get the oil off mine and went home.

A few days later, Jeanie and I ran into one of his family members. "You heard what happened?" the person asked.

"No, nothing," I said. "How did the surgery go?"

"There was no surgery. You had not been gone 45 minutes when the tumor came out of his body on its own!"

Some would say that is a coincidence. I do not believe so. I believe as soon as the man forgave, he opened the door for God's grace, mercy and healing to flow to him again.

Abandon Bitterness and Be Blessed

God does not want to withhold blessings from you. He wants to bless you, heal you, deliver you and restore you. His Word promises more blessings for His children than we could ever contain. Your trunk can be so full of His treasures, so running over with them, that when you sit on the lid, you still won't be able to close it! But only if you keep the lid closed to bitterness first.

When opportunities come to pick up offense, choose to forgive anyone for anything instead. Abandoning bitterness will bring physical healing and good health to your body, and it will strengthen all your bones.

Unloading Your Trunk

1. Healthcare professionals and psychologists often make the case for a mind-body connection between your mental state and your physical health. Can you also see a trunk-body connection in how your spiritual state affects your physical health? Do you know anyone who has long kept bitterness in his or her trunk? Has his or her physical health been in a state of decline, too? Not everyone who suffers sickness is bitter, but most people who are bitter eventually become sick in body.

2. We have covered many of the negative effects of bitterness and have discussed how bitterness opens the door for the enemy to attack your life. Have you ever considered how the opposite is also true? Forgiveness firmly shuts the door on the devil and has many positive effects on your life. God wants to heal His children, and "He is a rewarder of those who diligently seek Him" (Hebrews 11:6). Seek Him by forgiving others from your heart, and bodily health and strength will follow.

3. If you have prayed that God would heal a certain health issue, but you are not yet living your best life health-wise, reexamine your trunk for bitterness. Forgive, as the man with the tumor determined to do, then follow James 5:14 and ask the elders to pray for you and anoint you with oil.

10

Bitterness toward God

The Most Overlooked Junk

I have met both agnostics who question the existence of
God and atheists who do not believe in God, but what
amazes me is the number of people I meet who are bitter
toward God. Some people are angry over terrible things
that have happened in their lives or families. Others have
perhaps had someone close to them die, and they react by
blaming God: "Why did You take my brother?" or "How
could You take my mother when I was only five years old?"
Sometimes they figure they will "get even" with God if
they stop putting their faith in Him or even declare that
He is not there. As Psalm 1:1 says, they sit "in the seat of
the scornful" and are antagonistic toward God. Whatever
their reasons and reactions, they are mad at God. Many
actually hate Him.

Remember we mentioned in chapter 1 that some things
in your trunk might seem too hard to handle? Bitterness

toward God is one of them. It can be hard to face and is often overlooked or excused—or deeply hidden. It can lie far below the surface, beneath the other junk. You can unload your trunk of poisonous unforgiveness, fatal connections to your offenders, unfocused anger, bad habits such as complaining and causing strife, and all the other junk we have talked about. You can forgive everyone of everything. But if you keep bitterness toward God deep down in the bottom of your trunk, you will be sidelined in your spiritual race. That burden will keep you from going anywhere.

This chapter will help you search your trunk for this most deceptive junk of all—bitterness toward God. If we can determine how you came to possess it and clear up some misunderstandings, we can expose it to the light and remove it. If this chapter seems unnecessary for you, yet you are overburdened, read on. Maybe you have yet to face your anger toward God; this chapter will help you admit it. If this chapter seems impossible for you—or if you feel so angry at God that you are unwilling to be "talked out of it"—read on anyway. Many difficult things happen in life, and by urging you to blame God, the enemy's plan is to separate you from God and His benefits. The enemy knows the junk in your trunk will do just that, and something you read here may help you see how to get out from under it and get back in your spiritual race!

Admit It and Quit It

I have often given my congregation my version of counseling: "Admit it and quit it." You can see why our church has a ministry department staffed with associate pastors who are more adept at patient, tactful counseling than I am! If our people need intensive help with ongoing issues, they know that the senior pastor's office is probably not the best place to start. The first part of my version, however—"Admit it"—is exactly the place to start if you are mad at God.

So many people who are mad at God will not admit that they believe God has done them wrong. They may be afraid other people will be shocked by such an admission, or they may not want to face someone who will try to "talk them out of it." Honestly admitting that they think God has done them wrong is the first step in freeing themselves from this destructive burden. Job was mad at God and declared it in Job 27:2: "As God lives, who has taken away my justice, and the Almighty, who has made my soul bitter. . . ." No two ways about that—Job was mad at God.

Very often blaming our troubles or sorrows on God stems from a misunderstanding, and that was certainly the case with Job. Let's look at a few other statements Job made and uncover the misunderstanding at the root of his bitterness.

> "Therefore I say, 'He destroys the blameless and the wicked.'
> If the scourge slays suddenly,
> He laughs at the plight of the innocent.
> The earth is given into the hand of the wicked.
> He covers the faces of its judges.
> If it is not He, who else could it be?"
>
> Job 9:22–24

In Job's mind at this point, God is the author of every bad thing on this earth. Maybe that is your mind-set, too. Job was sure God destroyed both the blameless and the wicked. If a scourge came, Job felt God laughed at the suffering. If judges handed down poor decisions, Job said God had covered their faces. But we know from Scripture that God

117

does not destroy the upright with the wicked. He is not amused at the suffering caused by the plagues like AIDS. Nor is He pleased with the decisions of wicked judges. So if God is not at the bottom of terrible things, then Job demanded an answer to the question everyone who is bitter toward God asks: "Who else could it be?"

We have a little easier time coming up with that answer than Job. We have an advantage that he did not; he could not pick up a Bible and read Job 1, 2 and 3. Job is the oldest book in the Bible, and in the first three chapters ever written, we find that God was not making Job's life (and everyone else's) miserable—it was Satan. "Satan went out from the presence of the LORD, and struck Job with painful boils from the sole of his foot to the crown of his head" (Job 2:7). Yet Job was *convinced* that God was his attacker:

"I was at ease, but He has shattered me; He also has taken me by my neck, and shaken me to pieces; He has set me up for His target, His archers surround me. He pierces my heart and does not pity; He pours out my gall on the ground. He breaks me with wound upon wound; He runs at me like a warrior."

Job 16:12–14

God is after me, Job thought. *He's picking me to pieces.* But the devil was after Job, not God. In fact, God said to the devil, "Have you considered My servant Job, that there is none like him on the earth, a blameless and upright man, one who fears God and shuns evil?" (Job 1:8). God greatly loved His servant Job.

God greatly loves you, even when you are furious with Him. You *should* be furious with the things that pick your life to pieces, but perhaps your fury is misdirected. Perhaps it results from the same misunderstanding Job had in his mind. You should not be mad at God; you should be mad at the devil and mad at the sin in the world that allows him in. Once you have cleared up that misunderstanding, you are ready to follow the second part of my standard counseling advice: "Quit it." Quit targeting God with your anger and get mad at the right target—Satan—the author of every bad thing on earth!

Theology Made Simple

Though the Bible is true and the statements I quoted from Job are written therein, to avoid any confusion, remember that the Bible also states that Job's theology was *wrong.* The first thing God said when He showed up to talk to Job was, loosely paraphrased, "Job, you don't know what you're talking about." Job 38 tells us the Lord answered Job out of the whirlwind, "Who is this who darkens counsel by words without knowledge?" (verses 1–2).

Put another way, if we listen to Job's dark counsel and foolish words, we will walk in darkness as he did and perhaps counsel others to do the same. It amazes me that most of the church world does this very thing, picking up its doctrine of why bad things happen on earth straight from the faulty theology of Job. Many Christians have told me, "God gave me this cancer [or MS or other disease] because I needed to draw closer to Him" or "God let this awful situation happen to teach me a lesson." While we do often draw closer to Him through sickness or trials, and while He is in the business of turning terrible situations around to our benefit, God does not *cause* bad things to happen to us so that He can try to get a good result out of them. Let's take a little time to examine why bad things do happen on this earth.

In the Beginning . . .

In Genesis 1 God created man and said,

"Let Us make man in Our image, according to Our likeness;
let them have dominion over the fish of the sea, over the
birds of the air, and over the cattle, over all the earth and
over every creeping thing that creeps on the earth."

verse 26

God created you and me to have dominion. He created
us male and female and put us over all the works of His
hands (see Psalm 8:6). Genesis 2:15 gives us a more detailed
job description: "And the Lord God took the man and put
him in the Garden of Eden to tend and guard and keep it"
(AMP). That begs the questions, Whom was man supposed
to guard it against? Whom was he supposed to keep out?
That *whom* would be the devil.

You know what happened next:

And the Lord God commanded the man, saying, You may
freely eat of every tree of the garden; but of the tree of
the knowledge of good and evil and blessing and calamity
you shall not eat, for in the day that you eat of it you shall
surely die.

Genesis 2:16–17, AMP

Then Satan tempted Adam and Eve, and they ate of the
forbidden tree. When they gave in to Satan, they forfeited
their appointed position—they lost their dominion and
authority. They gave it away.

A few millennia passed, and then Satan tempted Jesus as
well. He took Him up a high mountain, showed Him all the
kingdoms of the world in a moment of time and said, "All

this authority I will give You, and their glory; for this has been delivered to me, and I give it to whomever I wish. Therefore, if You will worship before me, all will be Yours" (Luke 4:6–7).

Unlike Adam and Eve, Jesus flatly refused temptation: "Get behind Me, Satan! For it is written, 'You shall worship the LORD your God, and Him only you shall serve'" (Luke 4:8). Nonetheless, notice Satan told Jesus that the authority and glory of all the kingdoms of the world had been delivered to him, and he would deliver it to Jesus if Jesus would worship him. If Satan was lying about that dominion, there would have been no temptation for Jesus to refuse.

Who delivered that dominion to Satan? Adam. When Adam sinned, Satan took his dominion. "Through one man sin entered the world, and death through sin" (Romans 5:12). Satan took Adam's authority, which is why Scripture calls him "the god of this world" (2 Corinthians 4:4, AMP). Notice that is *god* with a small *g*. Satan does not replace God, he is just the god of this world system. And because he is, we live in a world that is far from perfect. Not everything that happens here is the will of God. If it were, every person on earth would be saved. First Timothy 2:4 tells us God "desires all men to be saved and to come to the knowledge of the truth." God wills that everyone be saved, but not everyone is because not everyone accepts His will for them. Jesus told us to pray that God's will would be done on earth as it is in heaven. If everything that happened here were automatically the will of God, there would be no need for us to pray such a prayer.

The Great Divide

"I have come down from heaven, not to do My own will, but the will of Him who sent Me," Jesus said (John 6:38).

121

Jesus' life demonstrated what God wills on earth. Anointed with the Holy Spirit and with power, Jesus "went about doing good and healing all who were oppressed by the devil" (Acts 10:38). Who oppressed everyone Jesus came to heal? Right—the devil.

God did not bring sickness, disease, oppression and bondage into the world. The devil did—the thief who "comes only in order to steal and kill and destroy," according to John 10:10 (AMP). If anything steals from you, kills you or destroys your life, it did not come from God. John 10:10 is really the great divide that shows us what comes from God and what comes from the devil. It also says Jesus "came that they [we] may have and enjoy life, and have it in abundance (to the full, till it overflows)" (AMP). You can tell right from this verse what comes into your life from God and what does not. All that steals, kills and destroys comes from the devil, and all that gives life abundantly comes from God.

Other verses confirm John 10:10's great divide, and many verses warn us not to be deceived about its truth. Interestingly, every time the Bible says "do not be deceived," it refers to an area where most of the church world *is* deceived. If you can grasp the truth in these next verses, you will be a step ahead of 90 percent of theologians:

> Do not be deceived, my beloved brethren. Every good gift and every perfect gift is from above, and comes down from the Father of lights, with whom there is no variation or shadow of turning.
>
> James 1:16–17

What comes down from God? Every good and perfect gift.

"But Pastor, what if He has a bad day?" you say. "What if He has a blue Monday?" It will never happen. With Him there is *no* variation or shadow of turning. God does not have bad days or bad moods. God is the same every day, the same yesterday, today and forever. He is a good God—all the time.

Good God—Bad Devil

If terrible things have happened to you and you have reacted by overloading your trunk with bitterness toward God, you have probably asked yourself the unbearable question: *If God is bad, life is truly hopeless—what's the use of even carrying on?* Bitterness toward God is always an unbearable burden—but it is also an unnecessary one. God is not the author of anything bad; He authors only the good gifts that make your life abundant.

If you have had a loved one die, realize that God is not the author of death. He calls death an enemy. Death showed up when the devil did. If you want to know what God is like, look at the Garden of Eden before the Fall. No sickness, no death. And after the Fall, God sent His Son "to undo (destroy, loosen, and dissolve)" the works of the devil (1 John 3:8, AMP). When Jesus comes again, the devil will get his due and be gone. And sin, death, sickness, disease, war, pestilence—all that steals, kills and destroys—will be gone, too. When God is in charge again, He will "wipe away every tear" from our eyes and "there shall be no more death, nor sorrow, nor crying. There shall be no more pain, for the former things have passed away" (Revelation 21:4).

Good God—Bad Devil. That is all the theology you will ever need. God is not your enemy; God is your answer. You are right to get mad about the destructive things that happen in life, but you need to get mad at the devil, not God. You have probably heard the warning do not "give place to the devil" (Ephesians 4:27), but there is one place you do need to give him: a place in your theology. You must realize that he is your personal enemy and hates you. He has an army of demonic spirits who also hate you, and they are all out to steal, kill and destroy so that you will live your worst life imaginable. If that realization does not have a place in your theology, you will think God is attacking you when your attacker is actually the devil. You will blame God for everything that happens.

The entire book of Job was about how he encountered a number of tragedies and blamed God. Job accused God of setting him up as a target and shooting His arrows at him (see Job 16:12–13), but the Bible clearly states that it was Satan who attacked Job. Job finally realized his mistake and stopped accusing God. He confessed, "I have uttered what I did not understand, . . . but now my eye sees You. Therefore I abhor myself, and repent in dust and ashes" (Job 42:3, 5–6). Paraphrased, that means, "Now that I've seen You for who You are, Lord, I know I was wrong about You. I am turning around and going in a different direction." Then Job prayed for his friends, whose theology had also been dead wrong, and God "turned the captivity of Job and restored his fortunes . . . also the Lord gave Job twice as much as he had before" (Job 42:10, AMP).

God completely turned Job's life around when Job got his theology straight and then prayed for his friends. Job was twice as blessed as before. He ended up with twice as many camels, twice as many donkeys and twice as many sheep, but think about this: He only ended up with the same number of children as before. Why didn't God give him twice as many children, too? Because Job had not lost the first ones. If you lose a sheep or a donkey, it is gone. If you lose your camel (today that would be your car), it is gone. If you "lose" loved ones, you have not lost them. They have died, but they are not gone. They are over in the eternal realm, but they are not lost to you. You will see them again! God even takes away death's sting for us.

Good God—Bad Devil. Theology is that simple.

Unloading Your Trunk

1. What was your first reaction to this chapter about bitterness toward God? If you immediately pushed away the thought that it could apply to you, yet you felt angry and hopeless, it may be time to admit to what you are concealing deep within your trunk. God already knows your heart; nothing is secret from Him. Admitting you have bitter thoughts toward God is the first step toward being set free from this burden you are no longer going to ignore.

2. Whether you just now admit you are bitter toward God or whether you already knew it very well, the next step is to quit it and make your burden light. (Remember my advice, "Admit it and quit it"?) Think about your "Why?" question that accompanies your bitterness toward God: "God, why did You . . . ?" Now reread the portion of this chapter starting with the "Theology Made Simple" section and turn your anger toward the true author of your trouble or sorrow—the devil. Then go before God and pray, "God, forgive me because I've been angry with You. Please turn my life around, as You did for Job, and help me keep my theology straight and simple: *Good God—Bad Devil.*"

125

3. Are you facing things that are stealing your joy, killing you physically or spiritually, or otherwise destroying your life? Not everything that happens is God's will; Jesus came to destroy the enemy's works. Right after the "great divide" verse, John 10:10, Jesus told us, "I am the good shepherd. The good shepherd gives His life for the sheep" (verse 11). God is for you, not against you. Make sure your heart is turned toward Him. If your heart is not His, or if you are not sure about it, read the section titled "Possessing the Ultimate Treasure" in chapter 12 and watch Him completely turn your life around.

11

A Clear Conscience
and a Junk-Free Trunk

Jeanie and I are outdoor enthusiasts, so whenever a chance for outdoor adventure comes along, our natural response is "Let's go!" One time, however, I felt different.

We were visiting my wife's parents in Palouse, Washington, and a friend offered to take us downhill skiing the next weekend. It was early April 1982; the mountains still abounded with snow. I felt a negative check inside about the skiing, though, so I told our friend, "No, thank you."

The story would have ended there (and would not have become a "story" in our family history!), except for Jeanie's response. Her jaw dropped and her whole countenance fell. "I've always wanted to learn to snow ski!" she cried. "Last year when we were here, I was pregnant with Samuel and I couldn't go roller-skating or anything! Oh, please, please!" she begged, batting her pretty blue eyes at me.

Her baby blues are hard to resist. I gave in and agreed to go skiing, but in my spirit was this *Don't do it.* Not a shout, just this little something. I should have prayed with Jeanie about it and listened to God. Instead, I became grumpy—Jeanie says really grumpy. My mother-in-law and I had a little tiff, and it carried on all week. I wasn't outwardly disrespectful, but I was not above doing little things like eating all the strawberries in the refrigerator and leaving none for Mom. That did not help my standing with Jeanie, and she says that is why she did not stop to think about whether I was really hearing from God about the ski outing. She figured since I was being such a rascal toward her mom, I was just being rascally about the skiing, too.

I felt as though things were not going right—not so much between Jeanie and me or Mom and me, but between God and me. All week I kept trying to put my finger on this thing in my spirit. I knew something was not quite right about going skiing, but I did not know exactly what. It was a little bit murky. I just could not pin it down.

Skiing—A Dream Come True

Saturday morning we drove up to the slopes. Our friend started to get out of the car, and I cried, "Wait! Sit down. We're going to pray." This much I knew: The unrest in my spirit all week had something to do with skiing. So I bound the devil, I loosed the angels, I pleaded the blood, I did it all—everything I knew to do! Then we headed out to suit up.

We started on the bunny hill, and Jeanie *loved* it. We skied all day except for a lunch break, and we kept moving on to more difficult slopes. Jeanie was a fast learner (she is very athletic), and she quickly caught on to the basics.

She was doing great, and the scenery was beautiful. Finally, although she was feeling quite worn out, Jeanie insisted that she needed to try the highest peak. I was content to stay below, but up she went with our friend to challenge the biggest slope.

Jeanie did not tell me this until later that afternoon—when she was lying on the emergency room table with her left leg badly broken—but Wednesday, Thursday and Friday nights before the ski outing, she dreamed about skiing. The dreams were about all the fun we would have, but they had one other thing in common: In each night's dream, she fell and broke her leg.

We did indeed have fun skiing, but on the way down from the mountaintop, the other part of Jeanie's dreams became reality. She got going so fast that even though she tried to slalom to slow down, she lost it—really lost it. Both bones in her lower left leg snapped at the boot top. Her injury was terrible! She was in a cast for *sixteen months*, and at the end of that time the X-rays showed that one bone had not knit together well at all. The doctors warned that at best the bone possessed only 5 percent of its normal strength. They said it would fracture again if not kept in a brace. They even discussed rebreaking the bone to start the healing process from scratch. (No way, but we will save that story for a book on healing. Jeanie knew God had done a work in her leg, whether the X-rays revealed it or not.)

Tripping over Spiritual Clutter . . .

You might think, *Why didn't God protect you?* He tried, He really tried. He gave Jeanie dreams three nights in a row. He took away the peace in my spirit. You might think, *But you prayed before you went!* Yes, I did. When you are out of

129

God's will, however, you can pray until you are blue in the face, but you are still out of His will. The Spirit of God had already borne witness with my spirit about *not* going. I knew something was there in my spirit, but I could not put my finger on it. The warning was unclear to me.

I am convinced that the reason I did not pick up on God's warning was because of the strife I let into my heart. I allowed discord with my mother-in-law and my wife to grow into offense, and I was so busy carrying offense that I missed the Spirit's clear warning. You cannot participate in strife, whether outwardly in words and actions or inwardly in thoughts and attitudes, without cluttering up your spirit and hindering your ability to hear God. I was too cluttered inside to hear Him—my trunk was too full of junk.

When your trunk is full of junk, your spirit gets cluttered. The definition of the noun *clutter* is "a confused or disordered state or collection; a jumble." As a verb, *clutter* means "to litter or pile in a disordered fashion; to run or move with bustle and confusion." In the natural, when things are cluttered, you cannot find what you are looking for. Have you ever spent an hour searching for something in your garage, only to give up because of the clutter? You moved things around, looked under things and behind things, but you got more frustrated by the minute. Finally you wasted money buying another of whatever you could not find in the clutter.

Your spirit can be cluttered with junk the same way. You are mad at someone who did you wrong in 1995, and you have more offense piled up from the situation with the other guy in 1998. Then she did that to you in 2002. Then there were the tiffs yesterday with your boss and the rude clerk at the grocery store. You have so much junk in your spirit that it is a complete jumble. Then when God drops something inside you, you cannot quite get hold of it. The Spirit of God is trying to bear witness with you, and you are thinking, *God is telling me something here. I know He is, but I just can't find it.*

That was precisely how I felt the week Jeanie broke her leg. That Saturday ski trip was a turning point for us. We both learned something about paying closer attention to God—Jeanie was not paying attention to His warning dreams because she was too distracted by the thought of a fantastic ski outing, and I was not hearing Him clearly because I was too distracted in my spirit by our little family issues and the offenses I had picked up. We both learned how serious the consequences can be when we are distracted! We dealt with the consequences of Jeanie's painful injury for a long, long time.

When your trunk is full of junk, your hearing is dull because you are preoccupied with tripping over the clutter. Don't break a leg. Jeanie and I know that story.

Hearing God in Your Spirit

The apostle Paul put effort into clearing out the clutter so he could run his spiritual race without getting tripped up. He tells us in Acts 24:16: "And herein do I exercise myself, to have always a conscience void of offence toward God, and toward men" (KJV). Notice Paul's wording: "I *exercise* myself." Exercise is work; that is why a lot of us skip it. We should exercise three or four times a week, but it takes so much discipline. It is not always fun, and it can be painful and inconvenient. Exercise requires us to work at something that does not happen automatically. Likewise, Paul worked at keeping his conscience free of offense because that is not automatic either. It requires us to check our hearts

131

continually to keep little irritants and bits of discord from cluttering our spiritual sensitivity.

Paul strove to be void of offense toward God and men so that he would have a junk-free trunk. His example is a good one to follow and we have spent several chapters toward that end—examining our trunks, talking about why it is important to get the junk out and looking at how we can do that. Now let's turn our thoughts to what we need to possess instead of junk. Again we take our cue from Paul.

In Acts 23:1, Paul addressed a council with these words: "Men and brethren, I have lived in all good conscience before God until this day." In 1 Timothy 1:19, Paul charged Timothy to have faith and a good conscience. It was absolutely vital to Paul that he have a good or a clear conscience. He knew that his conscience was the voice of his spirit, and that when God speaks to people, He speaks to their spirits. A clear conscience equals an uncluttered spirit, and an uncluttered spirit equals sensitivity to the voice of God.

Your physical feelings are the voice of your body, and they connect you with the physical realm. Your reasoning is the voice of your soul or mind, and it connects you with the intellectual realm. When God enlightens you, though, He does not talk to your body or your mind. God is a Spirit, as you are, so when God speaks, He talks to your spirit: "The spirit of man is the candle of the LORD" (Proverbs 20:27, KJV). Your conscience is the voice of your spirit, and that is your connection to Him.

The Spirit of God bears witness with our spirits. When people are saved, the Holy Spirit says to their spirits, "You are a child of God now. You are born again, you are forgiven, you are on your way to heaven." As Romans 8:16 states, "The Spirit Himself bears witness with our spirit that we are children of God." That is the first thing the Spirit tells you when you get saved—but it is not the last. That is just the beginning of a million things you will hear from God in your spirit. As you walk out your Christian life, the Spirit will bear witness with your spirit, sometimes about large things, sometimes about small. You are not supposed to be led by logic or open doors, feelings or emotions, circumstances or finances or the culture or what your friends think. You are supposed to be led by the Spirit of God bearing witness with your spirit.

Once your trunk is junk free, the key to running your spiritual race well is being led by the Holy Spirit. Sometimes the key to life itself is being led by the Spirit! At a leadership conference at our church, a visiting pastor shared a story about himself and another minister friend. They were at the airport, traveling home together after a speaking engagement, and about to board their flight. Inside his spirit, though, our visitor kept picking up, *Don't board that plane! Don't board that plane!*

That may seem silly. Flying across the United States is safer than walking across the street in New York City. But he could not shake that witness inside. He said to his traveling companion, "I don't think we should board that plane. Something is telling me not to."

The other man replied, "I don't feel anything like that! I want to get home to my wife and family. I'm boarding."

Our visitor was adamant: "I'm going to wait and take the next flight." He watched his friend proceed as planned. The airplane crashed and everyone on board died.

I believe the Spirit of God spoke to both His men that day. One had a clear conscience, and he heard from God clearly. I do not know what the other man had cluttering his spirit or what junk he had in his trunk, but he missed God's voice. If your conscience is not clear, you will usually miss it when the Spirit of God is bearing witness with your spirit. Sometimes you may miss God in something small, and though that is not good, it may not be too big a deal. Other times when you miss God in something large, it can be a really big deal. Huge. Having a clear conscience can save your life.

How Your Conscience Is Damaged

A clean, clear conscience is a treasure you receive instantly when you are saved, forgiven and made right with God. As you begin to run your spiritual race, however, there are some pitfalls to avoid along the way. Falling into them can damage your conscience, and when it is damaged, you will not be able to distinguish what God is saying to you. You do not want to violate your conscience and damage your ability to hear from God!

We discussed one of these pitfalls, picking up offense, in earlier chapters. The more bitterness you pack in your trunk, the more cluttered your spirit is, the less clearly you hear from God—if you can hear Him at all. That is not the only way to damage your conscience, though. Let's examine two other pitfalls to avoid. Then we will learn how to repair the damage if you have already fallen into one.

Closing Your Spirit to God

It seems obvious, but to be led by the Spirit, you have to be open to the Spirit. He truly needs to be Lord of your *whole* life. If you close your spirit in certain areas, it damages your conscience and prevents you from hearing His Spirit. Suppose you consider yourself timid, and you decide you will never witness about Jesus verbally to anyone. You think,

I'll do whatever else God asks, but I won't witness. That's not for me. Then God prompts you to share with someone, but you do not hear Him because you have closed your spirit in that area. Or suppose you meet a single mother who has financial problems. God desires that someone help her out, but you have already made up your mind about sowing finances. You think, *I put $15 in the offering every week for God's Kingdom. That's enough.* You are closed in that area, so what happens? You don't hear from God about blessing someone else.

You will miss God's guidance in areas you have shut down. First John 2:27 says, "The same anointing teaches you concerning all things." God wants to instruct you concerning *all* things, but when you are not willing to listen, you will not hear Him. It sounds a bit simplistic, but the way to be open is to not be closed!

In John 12, Jesus dealt with some people who were not open to God's voice. He was talking about His purpose for coming, and He said, "Father, glorify Your name." Then a voice from heaven said, "I have both glorified it and will glorify it again" (verse 28). God the Father spoke—literally in an audible voice—and what did people think? Some said it had thundered. Others said an angel spoke. Jesus told them, "This voice did not come because of Me, but for your sake" (verse 30). In other words, "It wasn't for Me—it was for you!" Yet most of them did not even know God had spoken, and they missed God's message for them.

I believe this is the condition of many of us in the Church today. We can be so spiritually closed to things that, although God is instructing us, we are not hearing His instruction. We even believe He is no longer speaking. We think He is silent, while in reality our own spiritual condition is keeping us from hearing Him. We must keep our consciences clear by being open to Him as Lord if we are going to hear what He has to say.

Having Your Conscience Seared

Paul listed some things people do when they depart from the faith, one of which is "having their own conscience seared with a hot iron" (1 Timothy 4:2). If God is saying to you, *Don't do that, don't do that!* about something and you keep doing it anyway, the Bible explains what happens: Your conscience becomes seared. Sin severely damages your conscience. If I placed my hand on a hot iron, the stink of burning flesh would soon fill the room. I would feel excruciating pain at the moment of contact and for a long time afterward. The pain would eventually recede, though, and my hand would heal. Then I could touch that seared spot, but the scar would not register any feeling. The nerve endings would be too burned to function.

When you subject your conscience to repeated sin, the same thing happens. The first time you decide to sin, your conscience shouts, *Stop! Don't do that!* That is God bearing witness with your spirit. You feel extremely uneasy because you know you should not sin, but you ignore your conscience and go ahead anyway. Then the opportunity comes to sin the same way again, and again you hear, *Don't do that*—but not as loudly this time. You go ahead despite some discomfort. The next time you are tempted, all you hear is a little whisper, *Don't.* You keep choosing that sin, not just for a week, but for months and maybe for years. Whether it is unforgiveness, gossip, illicit sexual behavior or whatever, as you repeat that sin, you will quit hearing what the Spirit is saying through your conscience. God has not stopped speaking to you, but your conscience has become seared in that area, and you cannot hear God.

Undoing the Damage

I know some Christians who feel that God never speaks to them. Others tell me He has not spoken to them in a year, or in many years, and that they rarely hear from Him. Do you feel that way? Maybe as we talked about God's Spirit bearing witness with our spirits, you realized that you have not heard from Him lately. Very often that means there is clutter in your spirit—there is junk in your trunk. Or you may have areas you have closed to God. Perhaps you continued in a certain sin until your conscience became seared. If you do not sense God's Spirit bearing witness within you, somehow you have violated your conscience.

If you want to hear from God again, it is possible to undo the damage. You can repair your damaged conscience through repentance and prayer. When you repent, you turn your back on sin and decide you are not going to fall into that pit again. The blood of Jesus will cleanse your conscience when you repent: "How much more shall the blood of Christ, who through the eternal Spirit offered Himself without spot to God, cleanse your conscience from dead works to serve the living God?" (Hebrews 9:14).

Repentance must be genuine. Genuine repentance means completely turning away from sin, so that if I had to choose all over, I would not sin again. There was one occasion when I thought I was genuinely repenting before the Lord. I kept confessing, "Lord, I repent, I repent."

Then I was still before Him, and His Spirit inside said, *No, you don't.*

I repeated more earnestly, "Oh, God, I *repent!*"

I heard again: *No, you don't.*

I started saying, "God, *I am just so sorry.* I'm sorry!"

This is what I heard next: *Yes, you're sorry—sorry I don't like your sin. You like it. You wish I liked it. But I don't, and you're sorry that I don't. But you're not repentant.*

Ouch. At least I was hearing from God again, but I didn't like what I heard. He said that I was more sorry He disapproved than I was that I had sinned! So I had to repent of that, too, because He was right (as always).

The Value of a Clear Conscience

A clear conscience is a priceless treasure. It enables you to live your best life because you can hear from God. You can be guided by His Spirit bearing witness with your spirit. First John 2:27 says:

> But the anointing which you have received from Him abides in you, and you do not need that anyone teach you; but as the same anointing teaches you concerning all things, and is true, and is not a lie, and just as it has taught you, you will abide in Him.

That anointing is the Holy Spirit, who abides in you. The Spirit came to abide with you forever and to teach you all things. Be careful here, though. Some people really take that "you do not need anyone to teach you" Scripture out of context. They say, "Then we don't need to go to church. We don't need to listen to preaching. We don't need anybody to teach us." God is not confused. He does not contradict Himself. Ephesians 4:11 tells us He put teachers within the Church. If no one needed to listen, He wouldn't have made some to be teachers. You should sit under godly teaching.

Yet consider this: No one can really teach you. A person can communicate information, but it takes the Spirit of God to put that godly information in your spirit, where His Spirit bears witness to it.

For example, you are now reading these words I have written. As you do, the anointing on the inside of you is teaching you about my words. You are hearing, *That's right, and that's right, and that one doesn't apply to you, but that one . . . you really need to think about that one!* Can you sense the Spirit speaking to your spirit as you read this book? That is one way the Spirit works to teach you about all things.

Here is another example: You feel overtired and overworked one afternoon at the office or at home with the kids, and you wrong someone by being harsh. You make a mean comment, and as you do, the Holy Spirit starts bearing witness with your spirit: *You were not walking in love. That was harsh and rude. Apologize.* No fun to hear, but it stops you cold. In order to have a clear conscience and hear from God, you realize you must exercise yourself to be void of offense toward God and man. You make yourself do as He says and apologize. That is another way the Spirit works to teach you about all things.

All things? you think. The Spirit will talk to you about all things—big things and small things, significant things and things you may consider insignificant. He will talk to you about your job, your relationships and how you treat your spouse. He will talk about your response when someone treats you poorly. He will even talk about how you drive. All things.

Having the anointing, the Holy Spirit, constantly working in you and teaching you in every area of your life is priceless. That is why a clear conscience is such a valuable treasure. The New Testament talks about your conscience 31 times (I counted). It urges you to have a clear conscience toward God and man. When you are carrying the priceless treasure of a clear conscience, your faith will function powerfully. Instead of tripping over clutter and missing what God says, you will be taught constantly by the Holy Spirit every single day. And the more you exercise yourself to keep a clear conscience and listen to the Spirit, the more you mature spiritually:

> For everyone who partakes only of milk is unskilled in the word of righteousness, for he is a babe. But solid food belongs to those who are of full age, that is, those who by reason of use have their senses exercised to discern both good and evil.
>
> Hebrews 5:13–14

If you will obey the Spirit of God, that voice in your spirit will become clearer and clearer. Every day of your life you will sense God directing you to do things, correct things, avoid things, even change things. Make sure you keep hearing the Spirit's voice by making sure to keep your conscience clear and your trunk junk free.

Loading Your Trunk with Treasure

After reading the preceding chapters, you worked through numerous "Unloading Your Trunk" questions designed to help you get your trunk into a junk-free state. By now there should be some room inside for new treasures. One of the most valuable treasures of all is a clear conscience void of offense toward God and men. Do you possess that? Check by considering the following questions:

1. Do you strive, as Paul did, to keep your conscience void of offense toward God and men? Do you examine your heart continually and let go of any irritation or offense that would clutter your spirit and prevent you from hearing God? Remember, it does not happen automatically. It takes work!

2. When you repent, are you truly sorry that you sinned, not just sorry that God disapproved? What would you do if you had to make a choice all over again in the same situation? Genuine repentance means you would not sin that way again.

3. If you feel God has fallen silent regarding certain areas of your life, could it be that you have closed those "silent" areas to Him? He wants to instruct you in *all* things. Repair your damaged conscience through genuine repentance so you can hear Him again!

4. Are you involved in anything that initially made you feel terrible, but over time has become acceptable to you? Consider whether or not your conscience has been seared by repeated sin. Ask a trusted friend if he or she sees anything in your life that contradicts God's Word and needs correction. Remember, "Reproofs of instruction are the way of life" (Proverbs 6:23). Let God's Word renew your mind about that area of sin, then repair your conscience through repentance. Stay sensitive to His voice by keeping your conscience clear and your trunk junk free!

12

Genuine Forgiveness
and the Ultimate Treasure

The Healing Song

They say that time heals all wounds
But I beg to differ,
For there are these hurts in my heart
I haven't got over.
Thought I'd forgotten
Thought I forgave
But when I look deep inside me
I still sense the pain.

I need You
To heal every wound,
I need You
To do what You do
With those broken in heart,
Torn apart,
Desperately needing Your healing . . .
I need You.

That song, written by Curt Coffield when he was worship pastor at our church, deeply touched hundreds in our congregation who had carried junk in their trunks for a very long time. Curt penned the lyrics while on an outreach to Bosnia, and initially the song ministered to those suffering from the traumas of war. When he brought the song home, however, he found it also spoke to those suffering inner wounds from spiritual battles. It helped people take an honest, if painful, look inside themselves and do the one thing that could help where all else failed—ask the One who is our Healer to intervene and to help remove the junk.

Getting past the hurts in your heart can be difficult. Curt's song expresses the very things we have been talking about: Time does not heal wounds caused by picking up offense—the bitter root in you just grows bigger. You can tear yourself apart trying to forgive and forget on your own terms, but that does not help either. When you look deep inside, you still sense the pain. To get rid of the pain, you first have to remove the bitterness from your trunk. Sometimes you need outside help with that. You need God. He can reveal areas of unforgiveness inside you and help you let go of them and forgive by faith.

Throughout this book, we have taken a long, hard look inside your trunk, that place where you carry the things closest to your heart. We have searched for many kinds of painful, heavy junk you might have stored there. We have asked some hard-hitting questions and have borne each other's burdens by walking together through ways to lift out that junk. If you sense any junk still left inside you, do as "The Healing Song" suggests. Admit that you need the Lord to help you let go of those final burdens. Forgive by faith, and ask Him to heal you completely, as only He can.

He will do it! No junk is too heavy for Him. As I said at the start, He is all for burdens being light. Jesus told us:

"Come to Me, all you who labor and are heavy laden, and I will give you rest. Take My yoke upon you and learn from Me, for I am gentle and lowly in heart, and you will find rest for your souls. For My yoke is easy and My burden is light."

Matthew 11:28–30

Jesus does not mean that you should carry only a light burden of junk. He wants you to be totally junk free. He means that the burden of fulfilling His purpose for your life will be light because you will be yoked up with Him. When you stay connected with Him, you will not be burdened down with unforgiveness. That will make it easier to keep your trunk junk free.

In this final chapter you will find four steps to forgiveness and four signs of genuine forgiveness. If you will follow Jesus' example and forgive as He forgave, peace will overflow your trunk. Your heart will be healed and whole again. Things will turn around for you, especially when you make sure that you possess the ultimate treasure—salvation. As you let go of the past and reach for all He has for you, you will begin to live your best life for Him.

Four Steps to Forgiveness

I pray that your trunk is more junk free now than when we started. I hope that you are running your spiritual race with renewed energy and that your heart is filled with peace. Continue to pull out any little roots of bitterness daily, before they take hold, by forgiving others whenever you pray.

Offenses will keep rolling off you like water off a duck's back!

To make sure your trunk stays junk free, here is a checklist of four steps to forgiveness. If you do pick up offense, follow these steps to weed out those bitter roots:

Step 1: Ask God to forgive you for allowing bitterness to take root. Unforgiveness is a sin. Freely you were forgiven, freely you must now forgive.

Step 2: Forgive your offenders by faith from your heart. No longer demand any recompense. Your forgiveness never justifies their sinful actions, but it does free you from the pain and from the deadly poison of bitterness.

Step 3: Put works with your faith by adding prayer to your forgiveness. Pray for your offenders daily, especially if you feel any lingering resentment. Your heart will turn toward them as you pray that God will bless them, and His love will rise up in you.

Step 4: Close the door to demonic attacks on your life. Bitterness opens a door to the devil, so you must use the spiritual authority you have in Jesus' name to firmly shut the enemy out again. Say, "Satan, in Jesus' name I take authority over every demonic attack on my life, over every spirit that has tried to attach itself to me or my family, my home, my business, my finances, my physical health or any other area of my life. I bind you in the name of Jesus, and I command you to leave. This door is closed to you!"

That last step is extremely important. Never leave it out. When you open the lid of your trunk to bitterness, the devil works overtime to load as much other nasty junk inside as possible. But as a Christian, when you forgive, you have every right to stop him. If you are not a Christian, you can gain the necessary spiritual authority to deal with the devil. Take some time to consider the "Four Things God Does Not Know" and the "Possessing the Ultimate Treasure" sections later in this chapter.

Four Signs of Genuine Forgiveness

How do we know if we have truly forgiven someone? When we forgive by faith and add the work of prayer, our actions and attitudes will display signs of genuine forgiveness. We examined Joseph's trunk in chapter 8 and found genuine treasures inside, treasures he used to keep bitterness at bay. Joseph demonstrated how to bypass bitterness, but he also showed us something else—the signs of genuine forgiveness. We can learn much from the depth of Joseph's forgiveness, which covered his offenders' sin, set them at ease, encouraged them to forgive themselves and stood the test of time. Does our own forgiveness run so deep? Let's measure it next to Joseph's example.

The first sign: Seeking relief from the famine, Joseph's brothers journeyed to Egypt and appeared before him, unaware of his identity. Even before making himself known, Joseph displayed the first sign of genuine forgiveness—he covered their sin.

> Joseph could not restrain himself before all those who stood by him, and he cried out, "Make everyone go out from me!" So no one stood with him while Joseph made himself known to his brothers.
>
> Genesis 45:1

147

Joseph cleared the room and dealt privately with the issues of the past. Pharaoh and the Egyptians never even heard about the cruelty of Joseph's brothers, and they eagerly welcomed his family. When you forgive someone, you do not spread it around by telling everyone else about the whole situation. You protect your offender's reputation. Proverbs 10:12 states, "Hatred stirs up strife, but love covers all sins." If you harbor hatred and unforgiveness, you will want to inform everyone about the injustice you suffered. Love, however, covers a multitude of sins. Genuine forgiveness protects the one you forgive.

The second sign: The second sign of genuine forgiveness Joseph modeled was wanting his offenders to feel comfortable around him. Joseph's brothers were so terrified when they learned his identity that they could not even speak, but he urged them, "Please come near." Then he added, "Do not therefore be grieved or angry with yourselves because you sold me here; for God sent me before you to preserve life" (Genesis 45:5). Joseph set them at ease, assuring them that he was not after revenge and that he saw God's hand in past events.

Yes, Joseph's brothers had beaten him, sold him and were responsible for his years in prison, but God used the circumstances to accomplish something magnificent—the preservation of countless lives during the world famine. Joseph wanted to preserve his family as well. Unforgiveness makes you want your offenders to feel terrible, to beat themselves up and feel like the scum of the earth over what they have done, but genuine forgiveness wants them to know that you love and accept them.

The third sign: Joseph displayed a third sign of true forgiveness when he desired that his offenders go a step further and accept themselves again. Notice his words "do not be angry with yourselves." In effect, he said, "Forgive yourselves!" He told them, "It was not you who sent me here, but God; and He has made me a father to Pharaoh, and lord of all his house, and a ruler throughout all the land of Egypt" (Genesis 45:8). Joseph did not blame his brothers for the past, nor did he want them to blame themselves. He wanted them free of remorse so they could freely establish new family relationships.

We all need forgiveness from God and from those we offend, but we cannot really move on from where we are unless we forgive ourselves. In unforgiveness, you want your offenders to wallow in remorse and self-reproach. Genuine forgiveness makes you hope they will let go of their sinful past and move on.

The fourth sign: Joseph demonstrated the fourth sign of genuine forgiveness when he kept on forgiving. More than a decade after he reconciled with his brothers, their father, Jacob, died. His brothers said to one another, "Perhaps Joseph will hate us, and may actually repay us for all the evil which we did to him" (Genesis 50:15). Again too terrified to speak, they sent messengers to Joseph with a story about Jacob commanding on his deathbed that the brothers tell Joseph on his father's behalf, "I beg you, please forgive the trespass of your brothers and their sin; for they did evil to you" (Genesis 50:17). Perhaps if Joseph thought it was their father's dying request, he would have mercy on them. . . .

Joseph wept when he heard that his brothers had not truly let go of the past. They came and fell down before him, and he reassured them:

"Do not be afraid, for am I in the place of God? But as for you, you meant evil against me; but God meant it for good, in order to bring it about as it is this day, to save many

149

people alive. Now therefore, do not be afraid; I will provide
for you and your little ones."

Genesis 50:19–21

Joseph put his brothers at ease all over again, even though
a new opportunity for revenge had opened up to him. Unforgiveness causes you to nurse a grudge until your passion
for revenge can be fulfilled, but genuine forgiveness stands
the test of time and keeps on forgiving.

When we genuinely forgive, our actions and our attitudes
show the unmistakable signs of genuine forgiveness. We cover
our offenders' sins and strive to set them at ease; we want
them to know that we accept them and we desire that they
accept themselves; and our forgiveness stands the test of time.
We truly let go of the past, and we hope our offenders can
do the same and move on to live their best lives for God.

Four Things God Does Not Know

The Bible tells us God is omniscient and omnipotent, or
simply put, all-knowing and all-powerful. We know this is
true, yet there are four things God does not know.

First, God does not know a single sinner whom He does
not love. He loves every single person on the planet, even
those far away from Him. You may have done something or
had something happen to you that you think created a rift
between you and God. You may think He is angry with you
and unwilling to accept you. Not true! You need to know that
nothing can keep you from God's love. You just need to receive
His forgiveness and make Jesus the Lord of your life.

Second, God does not know a single sin that He does
not hate. He loves every sinner but hates every sin. We
may categorize sins by whether we think they are big or

150

small, but sin is sin in God's eyes. Perhaps you are a Christian who has let a "small" sin take hold. You know in your heart that you are not where you should be with God, and you have drifted away. Hosea 6:1 says, "Come, and let us return to the LORD." You just need to turn around, repent and reconnect with Him.

Third, God does not know any way into His presence except through His Son, Jesus. You cannot pray or meditate enough, fast or suffer enough. You cannot live a good enough life. You may be like millions of people who say, "I try to live a good life. I believe in God. I go to church. But if my heart stopped beating and I stood before God in thirty seconds, I'm not sure if I would be saved or lost. I hope I make it into heaven—I guess I'll find out when I die." The Bible says you can *know* that you have eternal life (see 1 John 5:13). If you wait until you die to find out, you have waited too long. You need to know today that you are saved, and the only way to know for sure is to go through Jesus, who said, "I am the way, the truth, and the life. No one comes to the Father except through Me" (John 14:6).

Fourth, God does not know a better time for you to get right with Him than today. "Behold, now is the accepted time; behold, now is the day of salvation" (2 Corinthians 6:2). Did you know that the devil's favorite word is not some four-letter curse word? It is *tomorrow*. He will tell you to get right with God *tomorrow*. Remember the plague of frogs in Egypt? Pharaoh told Moses the frogs were too much. He would let the Israelites go worship God if Moses would only ask the Lord for some frog relief. Moses agreed and gave Pharaoh the privilege of naming the time when the frogs would leave. And Pharaoh said, "Tomorrow." *Tomorrow?* Apparently, Pharaoh wanted to eat frogs in his bread one more day? Squash frogs sitting on his throne one more

151

day? Sleep with frogs in his bed one more night? I have often said Pharaoh's answer is the most ridiculous verse in the Bible. Pharaoh could have said, "*Today!* Let the frogs be gone immediately!" But the devil always tells you to stay in sin one more day. He wants to plague your life and overwhelm your trunk with junk one more day! God will always tell you to come to Him *today.*

Possessing the Ultimate Treasure

No matter who you are or what else you have carried in your trunk, today is your day to possess the ultimate treasure—salvation. It is indispensable if you desire to live your best life. It is the pearl of great price in Matthew 13:45–46: "The kingdom of heaven is like a merchant seeking beautiful pearls, who, when he had found one pearl of great price, went and sold all that he had and bought it." Citizenship in God's Kingdom—becoming a child of God and an heir to all the riches of His mercy and grace—is worth selling your whole heart and soul to possess.

Are you in one of the categories I mentioned in the last section? Are you far from God, or do you feel that something has created a rift between you? Are you a Christian who knows in your heart you have drifted away? Are you one of those millions trying to live a good enough life who just are not sure they will make it into heaven? If you are in any of those categories, you need to buy the pearl of great price.

How? Jesus said you *must* be born again. You need to surrender your life to God and receive Jesus as your Lord today. When everything you have becomes His, everything He has becomes yours, and your trunk overflows with treasure. This is the most important decision you will ever make! Tonight when you lay your head on the pillow, you can know that you are saved and not lost. You can know that you are not condemned—you are forgiven.

The Bible says in Romans 10:13 (KJV) that whosoever calls on the name of the Lord will be saved. "Whosoever" means *you*. This will work for you. It works every time! You call on the name of the Lord when you pray the following prayer, and God promises you that you will be saved. You will pass from death to life. God will turn your destiny around right now, *today*. All you need to do is pray this from your heart:

O God, I come to You in Jesus' name.

I believe that Jesus died on the cross,
that He shed His precious blood,
and that He paid for my sins.
I receive Your forgiveness for all my sins.

I believe that Jesus rose again,
so right now I receive Him as Lord of my life.
I am not going to live to please myself any longer.
I am going to live for Jesus every day.

Devil, you just lost me.
Jesus, I am Yours.

Heavenly Father, I thank You that You have heard my
    prayer.
Thank You that, according to Your Word,
my sins are forgiven,
my past is gone,
I am Your child,
and I am on my way to heaven!

In Jesus' name, Amen.

If you prayed this prayer from your heart, you are a child of God, and you are on your way to heaven. Your life will never be the same.

Live Your Best Life for God

Ephesians 4:31–32 reads,

> Let all bitterness, wrath, anger, clamor, and evil speaking be put away from you, with all malice. And be kind to one another, tenderhearted, forgiving one another, even as God in Christ forgave you.

My prayer is that this book has motivated you to do just what that Scripture says. May your heart be free—may it be healed and whole as you put aside bitterness and all its bitter fruits.

May you continually forgive anyone of anything by faith, so that offense rolls off you and peace floods in. May you get the junk out of your trunk, let go of the past and go on from here to live your best life for God always!

Pastor Duane Vander Klok, who graduated from Christ for the Nations Institute in Dallas and earned his Doctor of Philosophy in Theology degree at Zoë College, Jacksonville, Florida, pastors Resurrection Life Church (RLC) of Grandville, Michigan.

He and his wife, Jean, served on the mission field for seven years in Mexico with an emphasis on church planting and teaching in Bible schools. They accepted the pastorate of Resurrection Life Church in 1984.

Resurrection Life has a weekly attendance of approximately 8,000 with five services each weekend and one midweek service. It is also involved with church planting. Along with overseeing various new churches, Pastor Duane hosts a daily television program called *Walking by Faith* and travels in the United States, Latin America and abroad, encouraging the Body of Christ with practical teaching from the Word of God.

Duane and Jean have three sons and a daughter: Joshua and his wife, Nancy, who with their son, Gabe, are missionaries in Mexico; Samuel and Daniel, who are presently working in the Student Ministry Department of RLC Grandville; and Stephanie, who is studying at Hillsong College in Sydney, Australia.

Everyone new in the faith is invited to contact Resurrection Life Church for a complimentary copy of Duane's book *Your New Life*. Visit www.walkingbyfaith.org to request a copy or call the Prayerline at 1-800-988-5120. The Prayerline is also available for sharing prayer needs.